To Fred,
For memories of your 1974 Summer
Holiday in Calgary,
With Love
Aunt Mary   Son
Mary-Lou, Jim
July 1974

INDIANS

as the Westerners saw them

INDIANS

as the Westerners saw them

by

RALPH W. ANDREWS

Two Moons—Cheyenne

Two Moons was a Cheyenne war leader with a long record of bravery. He was one of the Cheyenne fighters at the Battle of the Little Big Horn when Custer's command was annihilated by a strong force of Sioux and Cheyenne.

Photo—Curtis, courtesy Seattle Public Library

BONANZA BOOKS • NEW YORK

Copyright © MCMLXIII by Ralph W. Andrews
Library Of Congress Catalog Card Number: 63—18495

This edition is published by Bonanza Books
a division of Crown Publishers, Inc.
by arrangement with Superior Publishing Company

a b c d e f g h

Manufactured in the United States Of America

PRINTED IN THE UNITED STATES OF AMERICA

To those intrepid

white settlers of the West

who were caught in the tangled maneuvers

of the government

against the bewildered Indians

and had no recourse

but to defend themselves

against both . . .

this book is sympathetically

dedicated.

by RALPH W. ANDREWS

THIS WAS LOGGING—*Superior* 1954

GLORY DAYS OF LOGGING—*Superior* 1955

THIS WAS SEAFARING—*Superior* 1956
(with Harry A. Kirwin)

THIS WAS SAWMILLING—*Superior* 1957

REDWOOD CLASSIC—*Superior* 1958

FISH AND SHIP—*Superior* 1959
(with A. K. Larssen)

HEROES OF THE WESTERN WOODS—*Dutton* 1959

INDIAN PRIMITIVE—*Superior* 1960

CURTIS' WESTERN INDIANS—*Superior* 1962

FOREWORD

THIS BOOK could have been titled "We Were There." There is no better, more accurate source of information about an event and the people concerned in it than the recorded reactions of the people themselves. And in presenting a picture of the plains Indians it seems to me the best place to go for it is to the early settlers who had actual contacts with the Indians and wrote down what they saw and thought. In the words of the great Nez Perce Chief Joseph, "Let the people speak."

At the end of this volume is a list of books pertaining to the northern plains tribes which I read in connection with my research for this one. There are probably ten times this number detailing the life, customs, beliefs, warfare etc. of the Cheyenne, Arapahoe, Crow, Pawnee, Sioux, Shoshone and other tribes. Most of them have one point in common—the viewpoint of professional historians and writers who lived after the people and periods they cover. Few of these authors saw or knew the plains Indians when they were hunting buffalo, stealing horses, raiding wagon trains or escaping from reservations.

This author presents here a few accounts of people who saw, felt, heard and no doubt smelled the Indians whose lands they had invaded and usurped, whose lives they had disturbed and ruined. A hundred years and more after the settling of the northern plains these pioneer accounts lend authentic color and value to the tribesmen. In telling us of their experiences they utter far more truth about the Indians than we can ever find in professionally written material.

The search for these pioneer accounts represented some months and some effort and more was found than could be used. All of it was made possible by the splendid cooperation of libraries, historical societies and genuinely dedicated people. While many photographs, papers, letters and other documents are lost to the historian through the ignorance and carelessness of people into whose hands they fall, a surprising amount of data does come to these organizations and they are doing the public a great service by preserving it and making it available for study.

For the inestimable help they gave me let me here thank the staffs of the Nebraska State Historical Society, Greater Omaha Historical Society and Joslyn Art Museum of that city, University of South Dakota and its W. H. Over Museum, Pettigrew Museum of Sioux Falls, Wyoming State Archives and Historical Department and University of Wyoming. Specific credit for the photographs, journals, manuscripts in unpublished collections is given at the end of the book.

RALPH W. ANDREWS

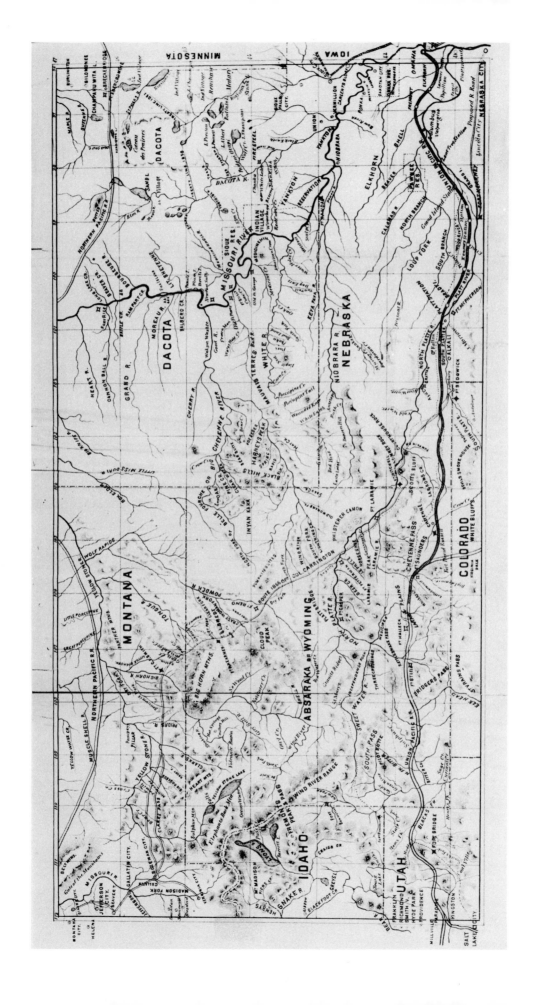

CONTENTS

Chapter One

"WE'RE GOING WEST, CARRIE!"

Wᴇsᴛ. Dreams and disappointments. Opportunities and tragedies. Fears and frustrations. But it was new country and the land was cheap. Dakota, Nebraska, Kansas—they were newly created territories where the free-spirited were going and growing up with the settlements, where a man could own and farm a quarter section and when the territories were made states, why a man would be made too.

"What will we live on, Aaron?"

"The land, the land, woman. We'll make our living."

"We work hard enough here. We'll work twice as hard on all that raw land. They say it's desert wasteland. And there's Indians."

"People'll say anything. See here, Sarah—the Pettison's have been in Nebraska Territory six months now. They ain't seen one Indian yet. Work? 'Course it's work. Hard work never hurt anybody."

It was man's world, a man's day. The Aarons were going west and the Sarah's went too. The children went. And the cow and the family trunk. They all went by river and wagon and train and stage—down the Ohio and up the Missouri, across country to Council Bluffs, Sioux Falls or St. Louis. With hopes and a few household goods they started new lives.

Friends helped. Ministers. And colonization companies. The emigrants went singly, in neighbor groups or formed bands on boats and trains when they found others going to the same place. And sometimes a German or Swedish colony or a religious sect already settled in the new country would send an emissary back east to bring out new recruits and sympathizers. A settler could preempt 320 acres or half that. He could homestead. A small cabin or sod house would do at first and people on adjoining farms would help the new family break up the land.

The shanties and little houses were hardly more than shelter from the searing prairie sun and shriveling prairie wind. It rained but not enough. There were meagre crops, some the grasshoppers didn't get. The farther west of the Missouri River the farms were, the farther away were the trees for firewood and fence posts—and the farther away were the next farms. And there were Indians. It was their country.

Crow medicine tipi

The Apsaroke or Crow medicine men usually painted their lodges according to visions beheld while fasting or supplicating the spirits. This tipi was painted dark red with various symbols. No man dared to so decorate his tipi unless as a revelation from the spirits.

Photo—Curtis, courtesy Seattle Public Library

The early western pioneers not only had little trouble with those natives but rarely saw them and then under most favorable circumstances. It was not so much that there were so few Indians scattered over the vast land but that they avoided the white men, their sage chiefs predicting that misfortune would follow any molestation of these strangers. The Cheyennes were shy of the newcomers, interested more in raids on the Pawnees and with their Arapahoe allies in fighting the Crows and Dakota Sioux to the north and the Utes to the west over hunting rights on the buffalo plains. The Mandans, Arikaras, Hidatsas and Omahas offered no problems to the white settlers except when provoked to fight by some misunderstanding or when some right was challenged. More often than not, in such cases, the fault lay with the whites who acted out of fear.

To the plains tribes of those early days a stranger, either white or Indian, was considered an enemy and he might be attacked if he was alone or in a small, unarmed party. Most Indians had a compulsive and economic need of horses and any man with one was vulnerable. Even the trappers and fur traders, generally on friendly terms with most tribes, had collisions and skirmishes with them, fully understandable when the principal payment for buffalo hides was whiskey.

Under the government's Indian Policies, alternately aggressive and vacillating, with the establishment of military forts on the prairies, trouble with the Indians increased rapidly up to and including the Civil War years. If there had been no widespread Indian menace before, there was one now. The tribes recognized the whites as enemies and it was fight or be killed.

After 1860 raids and massacres occurred every day. A settler might come back from town with a wagon load of flour and seed to see his house in flames, his wife and children murdered and scalped. Emigrant trains were constantly surprised by Indian attack. Soldiers on scouting trips were ambushed by war parties hiding in the bluffs and cottonwoods. Stages were attacked.

In the late summer of 1862, the Sioux rose in Minnesota and massacred a whole town and an epidemic of atrocities swept across the plains like prairie fire. A train of twenty freight wagons was set upon by shrieking braves between Julesburg and Fort Laramie. The Cheyennes wrecked a Union Pacific railroad train near Plum Creek, killing eleven men and carrying off captives and goods. Tribesmen living under treaty protection on the government reservations broke out to commit what depradations they could with a few horses and fewer arms.

All these outrages set the frontier on edge. Settlers fled back east or to the safer confines of the larger communities along the Missouri River. Those who stayed sought the sheltering arm of the United States Army and its military outposts or huddled together on the farms under heavy fire power. And then the army moved, first in one direction and then another, against the Indians. There was unrest and agitation everywhere from the Missouri to the Rockies.

And the pioneers, the settlers, the new westerners—what did they think of the Indians now? The Aarons and Sarahs had perhaps conquered the plains and filled their souls with satisfaction but had they conquered the people who had the plains before them? They were killing the buffalo on which the Indians lived. Were they killing his freedom, his spirit too? The Indian was friend and then he was foe—but who was he? What was he like? Let the people be heard.

Chapter Two

The SAWYER EXPEDITION

THE TRAIN was made up of 15 wagons each with three yoke of oxen, 18 trail or double wagons drawn by six yoke of oxen, five emigrant wagons, and twenty-six mule wagons belonging to the escort. As to this escort we may as well have had none. There was constant friction between the officer, Captain Winiford, commanding the soldiers, and Colonel Sawyer, commander of the entire expedition all the way through to Fort Conners where the escort left us. . . .

We left Niobrara June 13, 1865 with our cattle train in two divisions. Newell Sawyer, brother of Colonel Sawyer, and Jas. Harding, wagon masters, each of a division. There was a cook and a mess wagon to about every twelve men. Lewis H. Smith, of Fort Dodge, was engineer of the expedition. A. M. Tingley (brother of Rev. Wm. Tingley, then pastor of the Congregational church in Sioux City) was surgeon, geologist, and botanist. Chas. Sears of Onawa was secretary to Colonel Sawyer. Ben F. Estes, a squaw man, who had been a guide and interpreter to General Warren in his 1856 expedition on the plains was guide, and Baptiste De Fond, a Yankton Sioux, was assistant guide.

Samuel H. Cassidy, then one of Sioux City's leading men, politically and financially, was with the expedition as an emigrant. Accompanying him was a Mr. Edwards (a brother-in-law of Mr. John Lewis of Sioux City). A Mr. Merrill of Waterloo was also an emigrant and was killed by the Indians on Tongue river. Other men I now recall were C. L. Lee, a gunsmith in the early days on Pearl street, Joe Stager, a stage driver, and a gunman named McCurdy, a young man, Jas. Dilleland, who was also killed on Tongue river, Mr. Frazier, of Dakota City, two Edwards boys of Elk Point, a young man named Churchill from Monona County, B. F. Morgan, now of Minneapolis, and one Jefferson, from Wisconsin. These men were all teamsters as was I. Our wages were the same right through, whether we drove six yoke of oxen or three—$40.00 per month. . . .

A very important part of the expedition was the $20,000.00 stock of goods which the Hedges were sending out to Virginia City, where they wished to open a branch house in charge of Nat, the youngest of the three Hedges brothers. Many who were acquainted with Charley and Dan Hedges, their characters, and their business ability, never knew the boy Nat whom they intrusted with so much responsibility. He was nineteen at the time of this expedition and just came from school in St. Louis.

His mind was remarkable and that his wisdom was far beyond his years was proven to the men on that trip many times, for, as risks were encountered and as discontent with the command grew, this young man quietly guided affairs without assuming to do so, and without raising any conflict with the command, but the men saw this and placed great reliance on him. He shouldered responsibility and we knew that he felt that much of the success of this expedition rested on his shoulders. It was this shouldering of re-

*This account by Albert M. Holman, teamster on the
Sawyer Expedition to Virginia City, Montana, in
1865, is presented in its essentials.*

sponsibility that made him break his vow and leave the train to look for water, whereby he lost his life.

The expedition was nearly five months on the road reaching Virginia City October 12, 1865, having traveled 1,039 miles from Niobrara by Odometer measure. It was a long, tedious journey frought with many mishaps and many unpleasant incidents. We suffered in the sand hills for want of water. We found places we could not cross and went around. We went down hills where it was necessary to hitch cattle behind the wagons to hold back. We found that, if three or six yoke of cattle could not pull over or out of seemingly impossible places ten or twelve yoke could. We were corralled by Indians about twenty-five days in all, and six of our men were killed. . . .

THE TRIP BEGINS

We were mostly young, inexperienced men, who had never before even placed a yoke on a team of oxen, but who, fired by the idea of reaching the gold fields of Idaho, were determined to endure the hardships of the trip, in spite of fears of fathers and mothers.

For several years there had been a large emigration to Idaho, with Omaha as a starting point. Everyone was talking of the gold fields. Gold, gold, everywhere it seemed to us lads, if only we could reach Idaho! And now came the chance!

The people of Sioux City had been wishing to open a shorter route from the Missouri river to Virginia City, and believing that they could make the distance 500 miles less than what was known as the Overland Route to California, which followed the entire length of the Platte river from Omaha west to Salt Lake, had secured through the efforts of Hon. A. W. Hubbard, representing northwestern Iowa, an appropriation from congress to open a wagon or emigrant road from the mouth of the Niobrara river, in Nebraska, to Virginia City, which was then in 1865 a city in Idaho. The projectors hoped to make Sioux City the commercial center for supplying and outfitting emigrants for this route, just as Omaha was the base of supplies for the Platte route.

Col. James A. Sawyer of Sioux City was appointed by the government to locate and open this "Niobrara and Virginia City Wagon Route" and as he must have drivers and helpers of all kinds, we boys at last saw our opportunity to reach the gold fields.

It was the latter part of May, 1865, when Col. Sawyer, with his train, crossed the Missouri river at Sioux City and proceeded to Niobrara, where final details of the expedition were made ready. The government furnished us an escort of parts of two companies of infantry, paroled rebel soldiers, known as "Galvanized Yankees"—and a detachment of twenty-five soldiers of Dakota cavalry with a six-pound brass Howitzer, which made the path to the gold fields appear very easy to a courageous youth, whose only experience with the Indians had been in Iowa. . . .

One of the guides was a full-blooded Yankton Sioux Indian, the other, his brother-in-law, was a "squaw man." While those two men proved sufficiently familiar with the country to have guided a rapidly moving body of men, yet we found their knowledge of distance vague, and the distance to be traveled each day in order to camp near water, was a pony's ride, which might mean anywhere from ten to fifty miles. . . .

On reaching Long Pine River, it was found necessary to go up the river on the East side, possibly twenty miles, in order to find a place where the banks would admit of crossing. We camped on the west bank July 1st for that night, and the next day we broke camp and proceeded due west, hoping to be able to camp on the Running Water that night, but every mile took us deeper into the sand hills and the sun of a July day pouring its hot rays upon the burning sand, glistened so that we were nearly blinded. By afternoon it was impossible to go but a few rods at a time, it being necessary to stop often and let the cattle breathe and rest, for the poor creatures were prostrated and were suffering so for want of water that their tongues protruded from their mouths, and several of them died. The men, too, were nearly prostrated from the heat, and in fact, some of them were so nearly overcome that they had to be placed in the wagons.

Scarcely any progress had been made during the whole afternoon, and after waiting for the sun to decline, so that we might move in the cool of the evening, we hitched from twelve to fifteen yoke of cattle to a wagon, and turned due north, reaching the bank of the Running Water about ten o'clock that night. . . .

We crossed the Running Water about 325 miles from its mouth, and thence bearing northwesterly, crossed the White River and Het Creek. The Black Hills, looming up in the distance, grew more distinct day by day. Finally we reached and camped on what was known as "Old Woman's Fork," a river emptying into the Cheyenne, at the southern extremity of the Black Hills.

By this time, the soldiers accompanying us had become nearly barefoot and the officers insisted that they could travel no further without shoes. For this reason a detachment of twenty soldiers was ordered to go to Fort Laramie, which was about 100 miles south of us, for a supply of shoes.

At the expiration of ten days, the party at Laramie not having returned, we decided to proceed slowly on our way, as probably they would soon overtake us. No fears for their safety or our own were felt, as no Indians or recent signs of any had yet been discovered. Owing to this fact we were camping without taking the precautions necessary in an Indian country. While traveling together, the soldiers, with their mule train and the expedition proper, under command of Col. Sawyer, acted independently of each other, both while on trail and in camp. This was, to say the least, inexcusable on the parts of those in charge. . . .

Leaving the head waters of the north fork of the Cheyenne, we expected to reach Powder River in one day, but it proved to take a much longer time. For three days we traveled onward in this rough country (the Powder River Mountains), finding no water for our cattle and having for ourselves the little that each man had fortunately carried in bottles or canteens, for we had learned by experience that it was safe to keep water with us when we could. On the evening of the third day, our wagon master discovered a pool of stagnant water, and we at once hastened toward it, made a corral, and turned the stock loose. The poor beasts rushed headlong into the already filthy, slimy water, stirring it up so that they would not even drink it. They were so exhausted that it was evident the train could not proceed, and as it was thought to be but a few miles to Powder River, it was deemed best to drive the stock loose to water, so we selected by lot one-third of the men, who with the stock started from camp at daylight on a Saturday morning about the 15th of August. It proved to be about 15 miles to Powder River, over a very rough range of low bald mountains, and in many places the cattle had to be driven in single file in order to get along. At eleven o'clock they reached their destination, and the stock seemed to revel in the clear mountain water and the luxuriant grass of the valley. The guide, who accompanied the party, having gone up the river, returned with the report that there was a large body of Indians encamped about five miles from them. They had expected to stay there until the next day in order that the stock might be thoroughly refreshed, but a hurried consultation decided it best for them to return to the wagons, so they started back at five o'clock P.M., reaching us at camp at about midnight. When they told us that there were Indians in the near vicinity, orders were given to make an early start in the morning on the trail back, hoping that we might reach the North Fork of the Cheyenne again. That meant 36 miles back to the nearest water before the Indians should attack us.

The writer believes, that while up to this time, we had not seen any Indians, they had watched us closely for days, and as we were getting farther into these hills, destitute of water, and each day bringing us in greater peril, they were only awaiting an opportunity to surround and attack us in those barren hills, and our sudden retreat toward feed and water surprised them so, that only a small party of Indians made the first attack. Had the whole band made the effort at this time, I know no reason why they would not have captured our entire train. . . .

In his great anxiety for the comfort of the men, Nat Hedges of Sioux City, a young man about nineteen years of age and one who had an interest in a portion of the train, left us for the first time during the trip and started horseback to scour the valley in search of water. While the train was crossing the gulch, he had gone down some eighty rods below the crossing to a clump of trees, hoping that there he might find a pool of water.

About twenty-five head of horses had been turned out and were now quietly grazing down near these trees. When nearly half the train had succeeded in crossing over, a dozen shots were suddenly fired from the trees, followed by a succession of yells, and by the time every man had his gun in his hands, out rode about fifty naked, red devils making for the horses and riding along the west side of the ravine toward the rear of the train. Fire was instantly opened up by the teamsters along the line as they were nearer to the Indians than those in camp. The red men succeeded in stampeding the ponies, getting all but eight. The remainder of the teams hastened to cross the gulch, and at a call we all came together and the roll was called in order to see if any one was missing. Many of us knew that Nat Hedges was out and we feared and fully realized, when the first shot was fired, that some of our number had been killed. The Indians withdrew a short distance from us and were dancing and yelling as only Indians can.

A party was formed and marched down to the timber, and there on the bank as it rises from the ravine, was the naked body of poor Hedges. Seven arrows had penetrated his breast; a bullet hole was in his cheek and several in his body. His head had been scalped, leaving bare the entire skull. The lifeless form of our dear friend was sadly borne to camp and placed in a wagon, and we started on our way, a most sorrowful company . . .

THE INDIANS APPEAR

We were anxious to be situated nearer running water in case the Indians should prove numerous. The cattle being yoked and every thing in readiness, the wagon master gave the order to break corral just as the sun was showing its first bright rays in the morn. Almost simultaneously from several throats rang out the words "See the Indians over there," and in the short space of ten minutes, the entire surrounding hills were covered with Indians, there being not less than two thousand, some on foot and some on horses. A feeling of forlorn hopelessness seemed to spread over our entire party, not from fear that the Indians could take us, but because of our inability to proceed, or to cope with and drive them away. One hundred cavalry men would have gone through there or have been sufficient to escort our heavy train. The Indians were short of ammunition and guns, but had they been as well equipped as those Indians during the time of the Custer massacre, it is not probable that a single man of us would have lived to tell the tale. They at once commenced firing on us, but at a distance and using but little powder. The results were harmless. On the two highest hills, one North and one South, were gathered large numbers of Indians and from each group came the most hideous noises. They blew blasts from cavalry bugles, of which they had come into possession, danced, yelled and taunted us in a most aggravating manner. They proved to be the Cheyenne Indians. Some few of them could speak enough English to call us all the vile names imaginable, using profane language to embelish their sentences. With a firmly formed corral the front wheel of one wagon interlocking the hind wheel of the next, these all chained together and each heavily loaded, our position was impregnable to such an enemy. During intervals in which the Indians had stopped firing, we would hastily slip on the outside and by so doing, we soon had near the wagon a breastwork thrown up as high as the underedge of the wagon box. With three hundred cattle inside the corral we had close quarters, but felt secure against the Indians. We had food and ammunition enough for a three months' siege, but to get grazing and water for the cattle was our greatest concern.

16

One of the Indians' favorite tactics was to form behind some knoll at a safe distance from us, ride in a circling manner as close to us as they dared, and then at the nearest point to shoot directly at the corral. Naked, and riding bareback on good fleet horses, leaning way to one side of them, and following one behind the other, would ride in this way perhaps twenty-five red devils, some much more daring than others in venturing near the corral, but careful to keep at a good long rifle range.

To this kind of maneuvering we soon became so accustomed as to really enjoy it, probably on account of the exciting novelty that there was about it. Some times when this was done, we would open fire, but with only the old muzzle loading Springfield army muskets in the hands of inexperienced men and boys, to hit one of those Indians while swiftly riding, was about as easy as to shoot a swallow while on the wing. At other times when there seemed to be a large party gathered behind a knoll or in some gulley, we would venture on the outside of the corral with our six-pound brass Howitzer and let a few shells drop into their midst. Then with terrible oaths in the English language, they would rush pellmell and scatter in all directions, trying to find some safer place while we watched them, cheering heartily at their discomfiture. We would also maneuver around in order to give them a chance to attack us. Forming our men into different squads, we would make a charge on a certain place in which a number of our enemies were congregated. As we approched them on a run, leaving at certain distances a squad of men which were strung out for perhaps forty rods, the Indians would give way without firing a shot, but all the time slyly watching our rear, evidently anxious to draw us out. On no occasion did we go so far as to neglect having a line of men from the corral to the line in front. For nearly three days this kind of warfare continued, becoming quite monotonous.

About noon on the third day, the Indians suddenly ceased their maneuvering and put up a white flag which was a signal that they wanted to parley, and consequently a meeting place was arranged between the corral and the main body of Indians. They said that they supposed we were soldiers sent out to fight them and had they known the kind of party we were they would not have attacked us. We finally made an agreement and on our promising to give them a supply of provisions they said they would go and leave us. Accordingly, a wagon was loaded with flour, sugar, coffee and tobacco, about three thousand pounds in all. This was hauled to the flag of truce and there unloaded. The Indians quickly gathered around, and it was not long till the provisions were all distributed among them. We soon saw that they were in turn fulfilling their part of the promise and were now taking their departure.

Some few of our men had, while at the point of treaty, taken the opportunity of talking to the Indians and learned that they were very short of ammunition. They were so eager to obtain more that they offered us fabulous prices for powder, shot and gun caps. Some of them exhibited great rolls of greenbacks, and offered as high as twenty-five dollars for a single charge of powder. The young Indian who acted as interpreter claimed to be Choctaw. He was evidently educated for he was fluent in the English language but no doubt he was a Sioux Indian.

Two men, one a Norwegian and the other a Mexican, both belonging to our escort, had, at the close of the deal with the Indians, remained at the flag of truce. Late in the afternoon, after the Indians had gone, it was noticed that these two men were missing. A search party immediately started out to look for them, and just beyond a knoll a short distance from the flag was found the lifeless body of the Norwegian boy. Lying on his back with his breast full of arrows, a long sharp pointed pole was driven through him, pinioning him to the ground. The Mexican was never found, nor did we ever again hear of him. It is presumable that the Indians had induced the two to go farther out of bounds, and then just for devilish cruelty, they had murdered the Norwegian. Perhaps from fear of the same treatment, the Mexican had joined them. . . .

The next morning, no Indians having put in their appearance, we concluded to break camp and move back seven miles to the North Fork of the Cheyenne. Keeping well closed up, we moved very cautiously in two columns, but were only fairly started when we saw our enemies on both sides, and from concealed places they began to fire at us. They were very exasperating and annoying, but a few men, as guards, kept them at a comparatively safe distance so that we reached our camping place without any loss. . . .

We lay in camp keeping from twenty-five to thirty men on herd duty, as the stock was grazing as best they could, frequently being driven into corral upon the appearance of Indians, as about one hundred of the rascals hovered near by. They were undoubtedly hungry for fresh meat, as it seemed to be the cattle they wanted. A lookout was maintained from one of the wagons, and from this position one could command a good view of the grazing ground. Upon the approach of Indians, a yell of "Indians" from the guard would be taken up by the herders, and circling the stock, a rush for the corral would be quickly made. A deploy of men from camp would scare the Indians off, but as soon as the stock were put out again, back they would come. . . .

Leaving this camp, we proceeded in a southerly course and crossed the Pumpkin Buttes between the east and middle Buttes. Upon reaching the Dry Fork of Powder River, we found the trail which had been discovered by our two men. Evidence of recent travel caused much gratification as we had become greatly discouraged, but now felt that we were not alone in that desolate Indian country. There was not sufficient water for the stock and the next morning after reaching this place, about twenty of us started with the cattle loose, down the bed of this dry river, hoping to find a sink hole with water. About three miles below, such a place was discovered with plenty of water, if not wasted. It was here that one of the most ludicrous, and for a few moments, one of the most exciting Indian scares of the trip occurred. . . . when the sound of voices that seemed unlike those of Indians fell upon our ears. It took considerable of this kind of hallooing, however, before we had courage to look back. But when we did so, great was our surprise and joy on seeing white covered wagons and a body of U. S. Cavalry slowly winding round the point and approaching the place where our cattle were still madly endeavoring to drink.

ESCORT AT LAST

It having been nearly four months since we had seen any white men, aside from our own party, this was a pleasure far beyond our expectations. How eagerly we shook hands and plied questions, for it was such a great relief to once more be with some of our own fellow beings and to feel that we were safe from Indians. These soldiers were escorting a returning transportation outfit to Fort Laramie. Gen. Conner, commander of the expedition to Yellowstone country, which has before been mentioned, was now, with a large force, on his way to that place. . . .

We now learned the reason why the Indians had so suddenly changed their tactics and seemed so willing to leave us after receiving the provisions mentioned, at the time of our siege, described further back. Gen. Conner had by that time reached Powder River and his scouts having heard our firing, he sent a party out in search of us. So it was the approach of these soldiers that caused the Indians all of a sudden to want to "make up." They closely watched the movements of this party and we afterwards remembered that just before the Indians asked for a cessation of hostilities, a signal fire or smoke ascended straight up in the air, soon followed by another signal at another place after which the Indians made the proposition to leave us. The signal smoke had also been observed by the soldiers, but firing on our part having ceased, they did not find us. The writer has often wondered what the results would have been had not these troops been so near, though unknown to us.

Having completed the task of watering our cattle, we drove them back to camp, immediately yoked up and with light hearts proceeded down the road newly made by the soldiers. Reaching Fort Conner that evening we camped on the East side of Powder River on the edge of some timber. . . .

One afternoon the stock not being inclined to wander, the three herders stationed at this point of observation had gone below the bank and were lazily stretched out under the brush. In order to be more comfortable they had unbuckled their belts containing their revolvers, and laid them to one side. After quietly snoozing for some time, one of the party noticed that a few cattle had gone into the river. To prevent them from going way across, he hurried to his feet, rolled up his trousers and waded out into the stream to head them off. Having proceeded about half way across he was greatly astonished and terror stricken to see several Indians slyly crawling upon his companions. He had left his revolver on the ground where he had been lying, so all he could do was to yell "Indians," as he pushed on across the river and struck out for the stockade. The two other men jumping to their feet saw, to their horror, several dusky, naked forms peering through the brush. There were only seven of the hateful beings, and even if there had been a greater number, to run from them was more dangerous than to stand fight, but their first thought was to flee, and in their excitement, the two frightened men never thought of the three revolvers within their reach, but leaving them on the ground, they started up the smooth sand stretch of the river bar for camp. The Indians had, it seemed, left their ponies some distance back, and quickly running to the place, they mounted them and gave chase after the two men, who had by this time, however, a pretty good start and both luckily escaped the arrows shot by the Indians. At the first cry of "Indians," the garrison turned out on the other side of the river. We immediately started from camp to meet our men and soon had them covered by our guns. As soon as the Indians came in range, they quietly turned around and rode away picking up the three revolvers, and with these they probably felt well repaid for their efforts. . . . .

We followed Gen. Connor's trail, perhaps a hundred miles, then turned more to the left and struck the Bozeman trail, a route made that season by an emigrant party from some point off the Salt Lake route, as a cut off to Virginia City. This party was headed by Mr. Bozeman. This trail which we kept until we reached Bozeman City, followed closely along the base of the Big Horn mountains and crossed the heads of numerous streams which rose in these mountains.

DEATH OF COLONEL COLE

One day late in the afternoon, as we were just going into camp, on a stream which we had followed for a few miles, we were startled by the appearance of a squad of twenty cavalry men approaching on the run from around a bluff a short distance below us. They were the mail carriers which Gen. Connor had on duty between Fort Connor and the front. They had been attacked by a band of Indians and not being strong enough in number to fight them were retreating to the fort. Unexpectedly they met us and camped with us for the night. After reinforcing themselves by taking twenty of our escort, they started again the next morning to the front with the dispatches they were carrying. . . . .

The day, August 31, on which we reached Wolf creek, the East Fork of Tongue river, Colonel Cole, 6th Michigan Cavalry, who commanded the right column of the expedition of Gen. Connor, and Lieut. Moon, of the same Company, had preceded the train, for probably three miles, and had selected a camping place for us, on the west side of the creek. While waiting for the train to advance they rode up a bluff or ridge on the west side of the river in order to get a view of the country beyond. As they approached the summit of the ridge, they found themselves face to face with several mounted Indians. The Indians had undoubtedly been watching the movements of the two men and therefore had the advantage of them so that before they even had time to draw their revolvers, the Indians fired a fatal shot and Colonel Cole fell from his horse dead.

Seeing him fall, the Lieutenant put spurs to his horse and did not stop until he had reached the train, and reported the sad news to the boys. After reaching camp they went at once to the top of the hill, found the lifeless body of their beloved colonel and brought it down to camp. It was sad indeed to think that after escaping from the many battles in which this brave soldier had been engaged during the war, he should finally meet his death at the hands of these miserable, skulking, cowardly Indians. His loss was deeply felt by all. . . .

After breaking camp the next morning, we passed over the place where the tragedy occurred. This ridge was the divide between Wolf and Tongue rivers which were only a mile or so apart, where we crossed them. As we approached the river, which was skirted on both sides by a luxuriant growth of grass, young timber and dense underbrush, the thought occurred to many that this would be an excellent place for Indians to secrete themselves for an ambush. We even entered the river bottom where there still smouldered at the edge of the prairie and timber, several camp fires. . . . We had in our cavayard about forty head of loose extra oxen for emergency cases and also some which were crippled and foot sore. These driven by two herders on horseback, brought up the rear, and while they were in the river drinking, the air was suddenly filled with yells and shots. Out from the river, through the bushes rode our two herders, and also from among the bushes appeared one hundred or more devilish Indians, riding along either side of our line, and pouring a continual volley of shot into our midst. Some few of the Indians surrounded the cavayard left by the herders and drove them back to the east side of the river. Those riding up along our line kept at a long distance range, and apparently shot at random. Under the excitement, and with from three to six yoke of cattle to manage, it required quite an effort on the part of our teamsters to keep the teams in line and to close up the gaps as soon as possible, so it was difficult for them to return any fire; but the few men who were not drivers opened up as rapid fire as they could. Meanwhile, the head team swung around towards the center of the line and in a very few minutes we had formed corral, though a very irregular one, which was not to be wondered at under the circumstances.

We soon noticed that the enemy (Arapahoes) were gathering from points up and down the valley and from the hills west of us, to a place in the timber across the river. There a great fire had been built and from the bleating of the poor animals taken from us, we knew that some were being killed preparatory to a feast. In a short time the Indians had gathered around the fire and from the sounds of their hideous yelling and dancing, it was evident they were having a jolly time. This was very aggravating to us and we proposed to see what could be done to spoil their fun and interrupt them in their midday meal which they were enjoying at our expense. We hitched a rope to our little cannon and with twenty-five men started on a run for a position outside of corral, and toward the enemy. The trees concealed our movements and on reaching the desired position, the cannon was placed in position and we proceeded to shell the timber. The surprise to them must have been complete for with yells of rage and indignation they jumped up and began to scatter. . . .

So these Indians, when unexpectedly interrupted by our shells, rushed forth about as mad as hornets. The number of Indians had increased since the first attack that day to between five and six hundred. Thinking that they would perhaps be satisfied with the capture of enough cattle to appease their hunger for sometime and that they would not interfere with us if we should go on, we made the attempt.

INDIANS ATTACK AGAIN

So we broke corral again, formed our train into two columns and with a few men preceding and also a few for rear guard, we entered the low hills. . . . Arriving at the valley we wended our way between the bluffs and the edge of the timber in search of a clear open spot on the river bank where we might camp. The Indians were still following us on either side, occasionally firing at us from the hills and timber, and some of these balls struck the cattle with a thud that would make an ox jump but would not break his hide. We were now approaching the river bank some distance below where we had crossed in the morning. Here it was open prairie but with timber on the opposite side.

The Indians discovered our intention and about twenty-five of them rode rapidly down the valley on the other side and entered the timber opposite the point which we were trying to reach. This maneuver of theirs was within full view of the train and many of the teamsters wondered why a few of our men were not sent ahead to the high bank on our side from which elevation they would have commanded the east bank and kept the Indians out of the timber and away from the river. No attention was paid to the excited clamour of our men and we drove in two columns toward the bank. When within about one hundred yards of our destination, the party of Indians which we had noticed riding down to secure this position, opened fire on us. Our two wagon masters ordered "turn about quick." This was done. Since our trail wagons were in the right column they had to make a "gee" turn and in doing so the lead wagons with their six yoke of cattle were brought a long turn nearer the bank. This caused the drivers to be more exposed, for in managing trailers they were obliged to stay on the proper side of the cattle and use great care in swinging around, lest the wagons should be overturned.

The firing had now become quite rapid. The writer with his trailer and six yoke of cattle had now gotten fairly straightened out on the turn back and looked behind to see how the next driver was coming around with his "swing around." This young man, James Dilleland, had gotten his team about straight. His back was toward the Indians. Before I turned my eyes he threw up his hands and fell forward on his face. A bullet entering the small of his back passed through him. The driver behind also saw him fall and together we rushed and lifted the poor boy, whose life was now fast ebbing away. We hurriedly placed him in one of his own wagons, and resumed our places. His team followed without a driver.

We proceeded a little further and corraled only a short distance from the river. In doing this we made a second mistake, for this position was too near the river under the bank of which the Indians still held their places. Every few minutes a shot or two from them would go through our wagon covers or hit the wagons. An emigrant, E. G. Merrill, of Cedar Falls, Ia., who had accompanied us from Sioux City was standing near a wagon with one hand resting on the wheel, when a bullet struck him in the side. He dropped to the ground and expired in a few moments . . . We succeeded in getting our stock to the river for water and laid in what supply we could for camp use. The second night found both parties in the same positions.

It commenced to grow colder and we were obliged to remain as much as possible under the wagon covers to avoid the rain and snow. We noticed that the Indians were gradually leaving their camp and by night there were none visible. The rain had made the inside of our corral a perfect quagmire. Our stock were standing to their knees in mud and shivering with the cold. About midnight one of the occupants of the wagons was annoyed by an ox rubbing himself against the wagon wheel. He could endure it no longer so took a bayonet and poked the offending animal with sufficient force to make the animal bellow and jump aside. This caused the whole herd to jump and in an instant the frantic beasts had stampeded toward the wagon that had closed the corral and in their mad rush the wagon was broken down and over it went the cattle. This panic awakened us from a sound sleep and out in the mud we jumped, with our guns in our hands, fearing that the Indians had stampeded our cattle and taken possession of the corral. It was so dark that we could not see an inch before our faces. However, word was soon passed around of the cause of the commotion. We did not attempt to follow the cattle, for in our wet, cold condition we felt that we did not care what became of them, or ourselves either. So we crawled back into our wagons and spent the remainder of the night very uncomfortably. Early in the morning, in a driving sleet of hail, snow and rain, we took blankets and went into the timber recently occupied by the Indians. Here we found our cattle quietly enjoying the shelter of the brush and timber. We built bonfires and were soon drying and warming ourselves. Our cooks went to work and we soon had a call to "grub pile," which was very welcome indeed.

The Indians in order to escape the storm had taken themselves on its first approach to the nearest mountains where they found better shelter than the river bottom afforded ... We could see there was a good deal of commotion in their camp and we watched expectantly for hostile demonstrations. Imagine our surprise when in the middle of the afternoon an Indian came out toward our corral bearing a flag of truce. He was met by our leader and the Indian said that their head men desired to come to our camp and hold a peace consul. Consequently seven of their men came and were taken into the tent of Col. Sawyer, where he with one of the officers of the military boys, held a consultation.

The purport of their talk was about the same as that of the red men in our former experience in the Powder River mountains. They supposed we were soldiers sent out to fight them, but had they known we were only civilians traveling through the country they would not have attacked us. Many of them could speak English enough to be understood. They were very sorry for the harm they had done and seemed willing to do anything to show their friendship and good will toward us. When we asked them why they were still nearly all mounted with guns in their hands, they replied that they were taking precaution lest we should open fire on them. We told them that three of our men had gone to Gen. Connor for help and that we expected to hear from them soon, as they had been gone four days. We assured them that if they were as friendly as they claimed to be that on arrival of assistance we would be glad to leave them and promised them a present of a nice lot of provisions. Also in view of their good will, it was proposed that their seven head men should stay with us until our three absent men returned. They consented to do this and another Indian was called in. The information was sent to their camp and was evidently satisfactory to the Indians as they at once quieted down.

Toward evening a guard was formed around the tent in which the Indians were quartered and all went well until the following morning which was Sunday. Early this Sunday morning the Indians began to show signs of unrest and soon about two hundred of them, mounted, appeared on the edge of the woods. They were less than a quarter of a mile distant and they drew up in company line facing us. The attention of our Indian prisoners was called to this late movement on the part of their band. The cause of this, we were told, was that each man of our party had always with him guns and revolvers, and they concluded that were not acting in good faith ...

It was now a question of who would stand guard over the tent that night. We then realized in what a dangerous position the guards of the previous night had been placed, for each Indian had his gun and also a bow and a quiver full of fine stone and steel headed arrows. They had kept possession of these weapons in the tent and we determined we would not stand guard over them another night while they had such weapons which could pierce the tent and kill a dozen guards, without, perhaps even alarming the camp. While this question was being thoroughly discussed by the men a second time the Indians were straggling in, wishing to talk with their chiefs ...

In a short time about twenty Indians had again straggled into camp, ostensibly to talk with their chiefs. Col. Sawyer and Lieutenant Moon were in the closed tent with the Indians most of the time. Our men were ordered to keep away from the tent as much as possible. We came to the conclusion that we were now in a dangerous position for in the tent with the seven chiefs there were twenty-seven armed Indians who had avowedly come in for consultation. Not less appalling were the three hundred mounted warriors drawn up in company line with guns and bows and arrows ...

CHANGE OF LEADER

We were wrought up to a high pitch of excitement for this was a critical time and we felt that we must do something to prevent total annihilation. Some suggested a change of leaders. It was quickly put to vote and a new leader was chosen. He with a few men immediately ordered the straggling Indians out and away from the corral. We then voted on the question of disposing of the seven Indians held in our camp. By a close vote it was decided to let them go. It was argued that it would not benefit us to kill them, but would only make the others more hostile and awaken a strong desire on their part for revenge. So our newly elected captain went to the tent and ordered the Indians to get out. He warned them that if they or any of their number came again within shooting distance of the corral, that they would be fired upon. On hearing this the seven Indians took to their heels and ran as fast as they could toward their tribe at the edge of the timber line. Some of the more impulsive of our boys could hardly be restrained from firing on the retreating fiends.

Since we had acted so impulsively in electing a new commander, it was suggested by Col. Sawyer that another vote be taken, and so the men were told to step on either side of an imaginary line, but the verdict was the same as before . . .

After consultation with the men, our newly elected captain told our former commander that if he would destroy all but thirteen wagons we would proceed and fight our way through. The men did not feel called upon to sacrifice their lives any longer in order to protect a large train, which was chiefly government property, but with only thirteen wagons there would be men enough to afford protection to the teamsters. Seven lives had already been lost and there was no one who felt it necessary to risk his life in order to protect superfluous wagons and stock. Colonel Sawyer would not consent to the proposition of destroying the wagons, so the other alternative was to endeavor to get the train back to Fort Connor.

Accordingly we started the next morning in two columns on our back trail. We experienced no troubles from the Indians, but had a slight scare late in the afternoon. Looking back of us in the west, we could see a cloud of dust and an occasional glimpse of a moving body which convinced us that the Indians had taken up our trail and were following. But in a short time we saw the white canvas of a wagon followed by others visible at the top of the hill. By this we knew that instead of the enemy, friends were coming. Our fears vanished and there was a general hurrah and cheering. In a very short time a body of U. S. Cavalry galloped up to our encampment. These were followed by a company of one hundred mounted soldiers, Winnebago Indians, and seven commissary wagons. What a jubilee we held, for we had given up all hope of receiving aid, and to be so agreeably disappointed can only be appreciated in experiencing it. Captain Albert Brown, Company N, Second California Cavalry, with about forty men of his Company, was in command of this relief expedition. Captain Nash, of Decatur, Nebraska, was Captain of the Winnebagos. With them was Little Priest, Chief of the Winnebago tribe. He was a very brave Indian and a great fighter, and these Indian soldiers gave very little heed to any orders unless given them by Little Priest . . .

Our three men who had gone to seek aid had without much difficulty reached Gen. Connor on the Big Horn. He dispatched these troops to our relief with orders to escort us out of danger. These troops had been delayed in reaching us on account of the storm which has been mentioned and the condition of the roads prevented rapid marching. When the troops arrived in the camp we had just recently left, they could see by the still smouldering fires that we had not long been gone, so without halting they took up our trail and reached us as they had expected to do.

Captain Brown was not long in discovering the condition of our governing affairs. The next morning he called the men up and said that he was now in command and that his orders must be obeyed. He said he would escort us out of all danger from the Indians. His men and horses needed rest, so we spent that day in camp. The next morning we proceeded on our journey, going toward Big Horn. That same evening found us on our old camping ground on Tongue River where we had spent those thirteen long, exciting days . . .

We arrived at the Big Horn, September 20th, near the canyon at the base of the mountains. Here we halted for a day while the scouts were sent down the river to see if any Indians were about, but fortunately they discovered no sight of the Sioux.

23

Capt. Brown then concluded that we could proceed without his assistance, as we would from now on be travelling through Crow country and this tribe was not hostile. So on the following morning our captain bade us farewell, and with his soldiers and transportation wagons started down the Big Horn to rejoin Gen. Connor who was moving north towards the mouth of the Yellowstone.

After crossing the Big Horn we followed the Bozeman trail till we reached the Yellowstone, then travelled along the east side of the river for about one hundred miles, to the canyon and here forded the river. We crossed the low divide of Bozeman's Pass and arrived at the town of Bozeman without having any Indian troubles. Within a few miles of town we ran into a rail fence and the sight of this was indeed a glad surprise, it being the first signs of civilization that we had seen for six months . . .

From Powder River, west, especially after leaving the Big Horn, the hills and valleys were literally covered with buffalo, some of the herds numbering thousands. Many times we were obliged to halt our train for fear of being run over by them. At times while passing along near these animals they would be so attracted to us that several would follow along the side of the train, so close that the drivers could easily strike them with their whips. We were cautious not to scare them so as to see what they might do, and where there were only one or two they would even pass from one side of the train to the other, going between the oxen and the wagon. Every one killed all he wished to and we fared well on buffalo meat and other choice game.

Tipi on Big Sioux Reservation
near Sisseton, South Dakota

Photos courtesy W. H. Over Museum, (opp.) Rinehart, Smithsonian Inst.

Three Fingers—Cheyenne

*Sioux encampment near
Ft. Laramie, 1868*

*Ear Of Corn—squaw of
Oglala Sioux Lone Wolf*

*Chief Whirlwind—
Southern Cheyenne*

Photos courtesy Smithsonian Inst.

Three Crow chiefs, left to right: Black Foot, Long Horse, White Calf

Of White Calf—Unstai Poka (right above)—George Bird Grinnell noted he was a chief for about a generation, and when known as Feather, signed a treaty with Governor Stevens of Washington Territory. He was famous as a warrior, later devoting his life to peace between tribes for the good of his people. He had a great breadth of judgment, was kindly, benevolent and gentle. Under threats or bullying he was immovable yet quick to acknowledge his errors and modify his views. He foresaw the end of the buffalo, adapted himself and his people to it.

Indian camp on the Wounded Knee

Photos courtesy Nebraska State Hist. Soc.

Part of Ricker Collection on Judge's desk

Plenty Of Horses—Cheyenne chief

Little Robe—Cheyenne chief

Little Robe Goes to Fort Cobb

After the Battle of Washita, 1868, which resulted in many casualties among both Major Elliot's men and the Indians, and many Cheyenne, Arapahoe, Kiowa and Apache prisoners taken, Indian emissaries went to Fort Cobb to determine what terms could be secured if they surrendered and to procure news of the Cheyenne prisoners. These men were thought to be Little Robe (photo above) of the Cheyennes and Black Eagle, a Kiowa.

They talked with General Hazen who advised them to wait for General Sheridan, expected in a few days. Sheridan told the Indians they must give up the white prisoners and he would send General Custer for them, that they must return to their villages and warn the people of his coming so he would not be harmed. The Cheyenne prisoners, he said, would be given up during the summer at Fort Supply and he advised the Indians to surrender.

Although Custer related a slightly different version, he rode into the Indian camp at the head of his command and was met by some chiefs including Rock Forehead. The Indians said Custer was brought into the medicine arrow lodge and smoked the pipe the keeper of the arrows lighted for him. Rock Forehead told him he was a treacherous man and if he came with a bad purpose, to harm the people, he would be killed with all his men. The arrow keeper loosened the ashes in the pipe and poured them on Custer's boots to give him bad luck.

Rock Forehead was not far wrong, for Custer admitted that even as he smoked the pipe, he was planning on how to surround the camp, attack or capture it. He did not do so as he learned there were two white women being held captive in the camp.

Wounded Knee.
By George E. Bartlett.

The Wounded Knee fight which occurred on the 29th day of December, 1890, was a victory for the 7th Cavalry, known in history as Custer's old command; and many a soldier was heard to remark afterwards that that was the time when accounts were in part squared with the Sioux for the killing of General Custer in 1876.

Big Foot's band of Sioux left their camp on Cheyenne river and were headed for Pine Ridge Agency, S. D. To make a long story short, they were captured by soldiers and taken into camp near Fort Meade, near the Black Hills; but the Indians were not content to camp with the soldiers — they wanted to get down to Pine Ridge where the ghost dance was going on. So they took a hasty departure at night and got into the Bad Lands so quick that the soldiers were not able to catch them. They crossed Bad River into the Bad Lands, then into the valley of the White river,

Any Sioux whom his agent considered qualified for supporting himself was to be allowed to select for his own use a tract of land, the area of which was determined by the number of members in his family. Farming implements and utensils, oxen or horses, seed, etc., and fifty dollars in cash were also to be given him. Notices to acquaint the Sioux with

reaching which he was joined by recruits who

Original manuscript of account opposite

Chapter Three

WOUNDED KNEE

THE WOUNDED KNEE fight which occurred on the 29th day of December, 1890, was a victory for the 7th Cavalry, known in history as Custer's old command; and many a soldier was heard to remark afterwards that that was the time when accounts were in part squared with the Sioux for the killing of General Custer in 1876.

Big Foot's band of Sioux left their camp on the Cheyenne river and were headed for Pine Ridge Agency, S.D. To make a long story short, they were captured by soldiers and taken into camp near Fort Meade, near the Black Hills; but the Indians were not content to camp with the soldiers—they wanted to get down to Pine Ridge where the ghost dance was going on. So they took a hasty departure at night and got into the Bad Lands so quick that the soldiers were not able to catch them. They crossed the Bad River into the Bad Lands, then into the valley of the White river, then up the valley of the Porcupine creek. Here they were seen by Sioux Indian scouts from the forces of Pine Ridge Agency where two-thirds of the standing army of the United States had congregated to suppress the ghost dance. General Brooke was in charge there at that time, and Captain Wallace was instructed to go out and intercept Big Foot and his band.

The soldiers met the Indians December 28, 1890, and a peaceable surrender followed. Soldiers and Indians all proceeded to Wounded Knee creek and camped in front of the store which was located at that point and known as the Wounded Knee Trading Post. The soldiers went into camp and the Indians pitched their tipis a little to one side. Nothing occurred that night and next morning when the sun rose all were making preparations for the day's travel to the Agency eighteen miles west. But before starting it had been decided that the Indians should be disarmed. Many of them had good repeating firearms of the Winchester and Marlin make, and although a good gun is next to sacred with an Indian, they gave them up with very few words; for it was promised them that as soon as the ghost dance was stopped and they were sent back home, that they should receive their rifles back again. As the Indians were being disarmed the soldiers stood around them in the shape of a horseshoe; the rifles were collected and put in charge of

Judge E. S. Ricker of Chadron, Nebraska, died in 1926 after a long life as frontier lawyer, county judge and editor of the Chadron TIMES. *For many years he gathered material on the Plains Indians for a book tentatively titled: "The Final Conflict Between The Red Man and The Pale Faces" but death prevented any writing of it. A large part of the collection is made up of interviews with Indians, white settlers, former scouts and soldiers.*

George E. Bartlett, trader on the Pine Ridge Agency in South Dakota, spent his life with the Sioux and as government scout and law officer. He contributed many sketches and articles to Judge Ricker, including the one used here, and is the subject of the newspaper interview which follows it.

a guard in the soldier camp. A few of the Indians had concealed in their blankets some old pistols, but they were practically disarmed; but during some arguments between the soldiers and Indians some foolish Indian threw a handful of earth up in the air. How it started no one knows. But it is claimed the handful of earth was the signal for the Indians to begin the fight; but who would think that such a signal would be given by a band of disarmed Indians who were surrounded by five times their number of soldiers on three sides and a Hotchkiss cannon on the little hill closing the gap? But it started very quick, and the soldiers poured hot lead into the defenseless Indians without mercy, killing men, women and children. The fight did not last long for it was all one-sided. Soldiers killed each other in the cross-fire. The Indians had no chance to escape, and the only chance to fight was to get a rifle from some fallen soldier and use that. One Indian is known to have done that. He was observed by the gunner who was operating the Hotchkiss cannon on the hill. The gunner sent an explosive Hotchkiss sheel into the tent, which blew the Indian to atoms. A more ghastly sight I never saw. His entrails were scattered over the ground for several feet distant and his whole body presented a very much burnt spectacle; chunks of flesh appeared to have been pulled out of different parts of his body. Other Hotchkiss shells were fired at bodies of flying Indians who were trying to run away from the slaughter, but death was certain anywhere near where a shell struck. A shell struck a camp wagon belonging to the Indians that had been left standing in front of the store. In an instant the wagon and contents were a mass of flames. Women and children ran in any direction that a seeming opportunity offered to get away; but it was to no purpose; they were chased by the soldiers and killed. I saw five young girls run in the direction of a small hill, aiming to get on the opposite side and out of the range of the relentless fire. The girls were closely followed by mounted soldiers, and when they saw that their effort to get away was fruitless, they with seeming one accord sat down on the ground and quickly covering their faces and heads with their blankets, calmly awaited the death which followed as soon as the soldiers could ride up to them. Two little boys not over ten years old tried to get away by running up the road that leads over the hill to the west. One of the boys was a bright little fellow and said he was a half blood, his mother being an Indian woman and his father a white man. He could not speak English but told me in his mother tongue (Sioux) that as soon as the firing commenced they tried to run away and had run for the hill, and that they had gotten quite well away from danger, as they thought, when they observed a soldier riding a white horse coming toward them. As soon as the soldier got close he dismounted, and dropping to his knees shot both of the little boys. The boys fell and the soldier mounted and rode away, probably thinking he had killed them. One boy lived a week with a bullet wound directly under both eyes. The shot struck under the right eye, passed through sideways and came out on the left side, completely blinding him. The half-breed boy fared better; his wound was a flesh wound in the thigh, and he got well; but the other died at the Agency where I took them for protection and treatment. Other Indians ran wherever they could see an outlet, and after the fight (!) could be seen scattered over the hills laying dead, often with the dead bodies of their ponies laying near by, where they had been shot by the soldiers who had followed. It seemed as though they did not want any to get away. Captain Wallace who was killed in that fight was said to have been killed by a tomahawk; but more likely a shot from the soldiers opposite who fired across. Philip Wells, a mixed blood interpreter who was with the soldiers, nearly lost his nose from a knife cut; and a Catholic priest named Father Craft got a bad stab wound between the shoulder blades.

No one expected any trouble of this nature; and when I heard the firing from the hills nearby where I was riding on scout duty, I could do nothing but ride to the Agency and take the news to General Brooke who was in command there at that time; and when I rode up to his quarters and informed him that there had been a bloody battle fought at Wounded Knee eighteen miles away at 8 o'clock that morning, he refused to credit my story until I told him what I had seen; then he seemed to get very excited. The General

34

had much confidence in me, however, for when the troops first came to the Agency and the ghost dance was at its height, I was the only scout he could get to go to No Water's camp twelve miles down White Clay creek and at 10 o'clock at night, and inform No Water (who was one of the worst of the hostile Indians) that they must stop the dance or they would surely get into trouble. The dance was then going on, several hundred Indians participating, and in the light of the huge fire at night, the Indians with their ornamented ghost shirts on, made a picture that was calculated to be thrilling. I had a friendly talk with the old chief who knew me well, and left unharmed, where, if a soldier or anyone not acquainted had gone there, it would have been sure death. I returned to the Agency at about 2 o'clock in the morning and found General Brooke and the Agent, Dr. D. F. Royer, waiting with very anxious faces. I informed them what No Water told me, and that was, that they would not give up the ghost dance; that it was a sacred ceremony, and that they wore the ghost shirts which would protect them from all harm. Then followed the preparations for a siege. Entrenchments were made on all sides of the Agency. The friendly Indians were instructed to move in and go into camp on the creek above the Agency buildings, which they did, and the hostiles moved about in the direction of White river to the north, finally locating the famous Stronghold in the Bad Lands, as illustrated in the "Illustrated American" early in 1891, by a drawing of the Stronghold made by myself, and several nicely written and interesting articles written by Prof. W. K. Moorehead of the Ohio State University at Columbus, Ohio, whom I guided over much of that country on two different occasions.

Indians were constantly on the move; some coming in content with locating in the friendly camp up the creek, others joining the hostile forces in the Bad Lands; after which followed the killing of Lieutenant Casey near the Bad Lands by Plenty Horses, a Carlyle, Pennsylvania, graduate who after receiving a good education returned to the Reservation and joined the hostile camp. Lieutenant Casey was warned about going too far from the soldier camp. I have heard it said that if his canteen had contained water instead of whiskey he would not have been so reckless; nevertheless he met Plenty Horses in the hills and talked with him; on leaving as soon as Casey's back was turned Plenty Horses shot him, and the shot caused his death.

After all the disturbances had been settled between the troops and the Indians, later on Plenty Horses was arrested and taken to Deadwood by the U.S. Marshall after which he was transferred to Sioux Falls for trial. The trial was a long one and a great expense incurred by the government in getting witnesses; but he was eventually acquitted on the testimony of Captain Baldwin who declared that Casey was killed at a time of war and that it could not be called murder.

A herder was also killed by being careless. His name was Miller. He was surrounded by young Sioux boys who, after killing him, filled his body with arrows, and otherwise mutilated his body. A soldier's body was also found who had wandered too far away from his comrades. When found the body presented a horrible sight. The whole top of the skull had been cut off as if by a blow from a sharp axe. The brains were gone and the cavity was filled with snow; the hands were nearly cut off at the wrists, a little skin only holding them on to the arm, as they lay over in a drooping position, and his penis had been cut off and stuck in his mouth.

G.E.B.

P.S. I did all the work in the Plenty Horse case, being the deputy U.S. Marshall for that work and district.

Sioux tree burial near
Ft. Laramie, 1868

Sioux burial on poles

Chief Little Bear—Cheyenne

Photos (top and opp.) courtesy Smithsonian Inst.,
(left) W. H. Over Museum

Crow scaffold burial

Sioux burial on poles

*Crow squaw bringing
fuel to camp*

Photos (top) Jackson, courtesy Smithsonian Inst., (left) W. H. Over Museum, (opp.) Curtis, Seattle Public Library

Cheyenne Chief Wolf Robe

Chief Bloody Mouth—
Hunkpapa Sioux

Photos (left) Rinehart and (opp.) Gardner,
courtesy Smithsonian Inst.

The Cheyennes Put to Rout

In October, 1864, while government men were meeting with Cheyenne and Arapahoe leaders in Denver in an effort to effect some peace, General Blunt was marching from Fort Larned up Pawnee Creek, a tributary of the Arkansas River, with a strong force of cavalry. His advance guard under Major Anthony suddenly saw and attacked a small party of Cheyennes.

Other Indians immediately came up, Wolf Robe (photo above) among them. The cavalry guard withdrew to safety and would probably have fled in panic except for the counsel of the Delaware and Shawnee scouts who advised the soldiers to take up a defensive position on a hill. The Cheyennes kept circling around the base, shooting arrows and stirring up great clouds of dust.

As General Blunt rode up with his force, the fifty or more Cheyennes fell back to prepare for a major battle. Blunt pursued them and the Cheyennes fled back to their camp, ordered the women to take down all the lodges and pack all goods, and were presently in full flight. The troops kept after them for several days but were unable to move fast enough to overtake them.

This incident points up the doubt put in the minds of the Cheyenne Indians. While their chiefs were in Denver trying to make peace, a small band of them had been attacked by Anthony's troops and a village put to flight. Such flagrant abuse of privilege was ever the cause of Indian uprisings and atrocities.

40

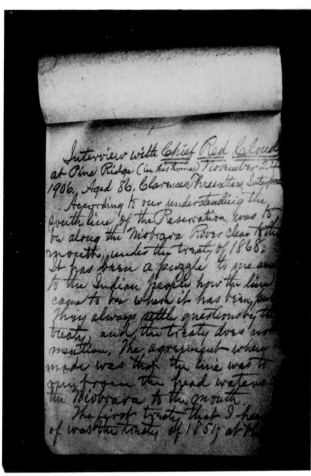

Original manuscript of Red Cloud interview

Sioux Chief Red Cloud

Photos (left) courtesy Nebraska State Hist. Soc., (right) W. H. Over Museum

Red Cloud

The famous Oglala Sioux Chief Red Cloud was born in 1822, receiving his name in recognition of bravery from his father after the latter's death. Earlier he was known as Two Arrows, getting medicine from his brother-in-law Nachili which was tied in a little deerskin bag which he rubbed over his body before going to war, a medicine regarded by the tribe as very potent.

Red Cloud first gained the attention of white men by killing Captain Fetterman and eighty soldiers in 1866 at Fort Phil Kearny. The following year he led a large party, 2500 or more, in an attack on a wood train at the same post but was repulsed with great loss. After the abandonment of that fort, he became the head chief of the Oglala Sioux. Red Cloud was prevented from entering the Custer fight by the action of General Mackenzie who disarmed him and his entire camp.

42

Chapter Four

SIOUX and THEIR CUSTOMS

Mr. GEORGE E. BARTLETT, a trader in the Pine Ridge Reservation, was in the city yesterday on his way east for business purposes. He called on his old friend Mr. Emery, of the Omaha detective association, and there a *Bee* reporter had the pleasure of an hour's chat with him. Mr. Bartlett is yet a young man, but his life from early youth has been spent among the Sioux, as he is as well acquainted with their customs, language and history as a member of the tribe. Mr. Bartlett is not prejudiced by any interests to distort facts, and as he is an intelligent and observing man, he affords more facts of interest and importance relative to the national wards of the Pine Ridge and Rosebud agencies than anyone recently interviewed from those frontier districts.

"The Fremont, Elkhorn & Missouri Valley railway extension," said he in reply to a question upon that point, "has proven to the agency the most beneficial step yet taken in that region. The line at Gordon is only twenty-six miles south of the agency, and freighting from that point is not the tremendous job that hauling supplies over the hundreds of miles of plains formerly was. It is an interesting fact, perhaps not generally known, that Indians are paid a liberal toll for freighting their own rations into the reservation. There are now about 8000 Sioux and 2000 Pawnees on the Pine Ridge, and they are all reveling to fatness in the liberal government bounty. The cash annuities are large, and the clothing, rations, blankets, and household goods are sufficient for their comfort. Game abounds on the reservation, and every month two hundred and fifty cattle of butcher stock are driven in. These the Indians kill and eat, selling the hides for $3.00 to the traders. The Indians do not live in one great body about the agency as many suppose, but are scattered over the reservation in camps and small communities, five, ten, twenty and even fifty miles from the agency. Each of these small towns, as you may choose to call them, set up some male member whom they call chief, but his sway is a mockery of the dominion of the warrior kinds who in aboriginal times spread the glory and terror of the Sioux nation from the great rivers to the mountains."

"How about Red Cloud and his claim to the chieftancy, and on that point tell me something about his trouble with Dr. McGillicuddy," asked the reporter.

"Red Cloud is a weak-minded old scamp and his assumption of leadership is discountenanced by the large body of the Sioux. He has the following of a few Indians and a number of 'squaw men.' These last are whites who settle among the Indians and marry squaws. They are all almost without exception shiftless, worthless knaves, although I know one or two old fellows who frequently come into my store who are harmless, good natured men. But the 'squaw men' as a class are a troublesome lot, and it is they who have incited old Red Cloud to many of his 'kicks' against the agent. McGilli-

This article is transcribed from a handwritten manuscript in the Ricker Collection, which in turn was copied from a feature in the Omaha BEE *of unknown date, presumably about 1886 or 1887.*

cuddy has a bad opinion of the 'squaw men' and has given them frequent occasion to understand his sentiments. They therefore do not love him, and have found in Red Cloud a pliant tool for annoying the doctor. . . . All the traders like McGillicuddy and believe him to be earnestly and singly devoted to interests of the Indians and the promotion of the peace, prosperity and growing civilization which he has established since entering his office."

Mr. Bartlett had with him a number of photographs of scenes about the reservation as well as the likenesses of all the distinguished Sioux of both Pine Ridge and Rosebud agencies. A glance through the album with explanatory remarks on each portrait by Mr. Bartlett is full of interest. The photos were taken by an itinerant artist who worked to his monetary profit upon the vanity of the Indians, but the work is very good. . . .

Stands First graced a card in his native costume. This gentleman is noteworthy from the fact that he has so compromised his credit that he can't get 'tick.' He is a confidence man and works all new arrivals, white or red, with some racket that is always damaging to the pockets of his subject. . . .

"How do Indians receive such singular and significant names?" Bartlett was asked.

"The ceremony of christening is not very elaborate nor the influences of name selection always the same. Differing signally from their white brothers, they do not worry for months beforehand for a suitable name for the 'little angel.' It frequently happens that a pappoose is far advanced in years before the matter of his name is thought of, and then for some performance or exploit or suggestive event he may be named at once. For instance, the great and brave Sioux, Young Man Afraid Of His Horses, was dubbed that for shying, when a child, from some fiery cayuse his stern father was forcing him to mount. Again it occurs that a child is christened on the moment of his birth from some coincident circumstance. For example, at the nativity of Bear Running Through The Woods, his father may have glanced out of the wigwam door and seen a grizzly scampering through the adjacent timber, a sight inspiring a title for his heir. Rain In The Face, the Sioux who is said to have killed Custer in that terrible fight on the Little Big Horn, was born in bad weather, and a gust of wind blowing in a spray of rain wet the face of the newborn infant, a most apt suggestion for his name. One remarkable feature of Indian nomenclature is that the selections are frequently unchaste and at times shockingly indecent. Although they have instincts of modesty, such as discountenance of exposure of person or lewdness of any character, there is no such thing as vulgarity in the speech of the Indian. All themes are open to mention in the presence of both men and women, and matters on which we would feel the utmost delicacy are freely discussed between them. The propriety of this is insured by the innocence in which custom allows it. The Indian knows nothing of the salacious, filthy converse largely common to his more enlightened white brother. He cannot appreciate the vicious pleasure excited by a vulgar yarn, for to him the subject is matter-of-fact and not under the ban of indecency. However, you would have to laugh amid your blushes if a list of some of these household titles were read off to you. Their mentionable names are peculiar enough. There is Walks Under The Ground, Kills The Enemy Alone, Not Afraid Of Pawnee, Poor Bear, Hunts His Horses, Coyote Howls To The Moon, Bull With One Horn, Eats Raw Meat, Builds His House By The River, Don't Like His Pipe, Climbs Cottonwood Tree and countless other such long and outlandish names. Their length is accounted for by the peculiar construction of the language. Rest assured the names are not so long in the Sioux tongue. It frequently occurs that one short word expresses all there is in the translation. Thus, if a chief on a trail wishes to leave orders behind him for a following detachment, he can write it on a piece of bark made fast to a pole, which he plants on the trail. In so doing he may leave but one word, and yet those few letters can convey an order to 'follow the picked trail to the third butte and turn to the south two hours' ride, where I will join you.' That is the reason that the Indians frequently have such long names when translated. Were they so unwieldy in their own speech they would not be made use of any more than among us."

Yellow Bear—Sioux

Little Hawk—Sioux

Red Dog's village—
Sioux, 1876

Young Man Afraid Of His Horses
in his South Dakota camp. Left to right: daughter, mother, Young Man
Afraid Of His Horses, granddaughter, two wives.

In Oglala Sioux the name was "Ta sun ke kokipapi hok silan," which actually in English was "Boy afraid of his horses," at the same time carrying a meaning similar to the English word "junior" as applied to a son having his father's full name. He was always friendly toward the whites, taking no part in troubles between them and the Sioux, was never inclined to be quarrelsome. His camp in the latter days was on White Clay Creek, about nine miles north of Pine Ridge, South Dakota, where he lived a quiet, peaceful life with his followers, of whom he had a great many.

Photos (above and bottom opp.) courtesy Nebraska State Hist. Soc.,
(top, opp.) Wyoming State Archives

Sioux of three tribes

*Left to right: Spotted Tail, Brule murdered by Cross; Roman Nose, Minneconjou;
Young Man Afraid Of His Horses, Oglala; Lone Horn; Whistling Elk; Pipe. Indian
at right unidentified.*

Young Man Afraid Of His Horses is third from left in group below

Frame of sweat lodge

Feather Head—Arapahoe squaw

Photos (top) courtesy U. of Wyoming, (left) Nebraska State Hist. Soc.

Chapter Five

TO TAKE
A SCALP

I T HAPPENED many times. Usually against a background of desolation and sage brush an Indian stood over his slain enemy. He grabbed the scalp and with two quick circular thrusts his knife loosened the skin. With his feet against the dead man's shoulder, he pulled until the scalp came loose with a characteristic flop. It was the act of a savage and many Indians of North America were guilty of such a universally condemned custom.

Little has really been said and much has been misunderstood about scalping. It is usually the Plains Indians of America that one associates with scalping. However, the custom was not unknown to the Old World where it was practiced by the Scythians. The custom of scalping was originally involved with decapitation or the severing of other parts of the body, the parts being considered as war trophies. The shrinking of heads by the Jivaro Indians of Ecquador was an example of this. The taking of the scalp rather than the head was probably a practical approach to the matter. The scalp was much lighter and easier to decorate. In America the custom was originally confined to a limited area of the eastern United States and the lower St. Lawrence region. It was actually unknown in the Plains area until comparatively recent times. Scalping was rare in Central and South America and was not practiced to any extent in the Canadian Northwest nor along the Pacific Coast.

It was the bounty system beginning with our colonial and the more recent governments that actually stimulated the spread of scalping. If you had a good day in 1724 and came staggering home with an Indian scalp, the colony of Massachusetts gave you one hundred pounds of sterling. This was the equivalent of five hundred dollars. In 1755 the same government gave you forty pounds of sterling for a male Indian scalp over twelve years of age and twenty pounds of sterling for a female or child scalp.

The Plains Indian was probably studied or observed first hand to a greater extent than other Indian groups. Those who spent considerable time in the West differed in their opinion as to why the Indian scalped his enemy. Francis Parkman thought it represented a barbarian who had or needed little meaning or reason for his actions. George Catlin, the early painter of the Plains Indian, felt that the Indian had definite reasons which motivated his actions. Catlin said the Indian, like anyone else, had to establish his position in society and that he used the scalp as one of the records or certificates of achievement. It stood for bravery and its value lay in its ability to impress his fellow warrior. At any rate, scalping was handed down as a regulation or part of the Indian's society which was never questioned.

Some thought that the number of scalps obtained greatly aided the aspiring young warrior to boost his standing in the community. Most everyone agreed it helped, but there were other "coups" or acts of bravery. Catlin, in describing his paintings of scalp poles, implied there was a typical "keeping up with the Joneses" approach. The chief put up his scalp pole first and immediately the other warriors were expected to do the same.

Written by Everett L. Ellis in ANNALS OF WYOMING,
Vol. 31, October 1959. No. 2.

Everyone looked at the scalp poles and counted the number of scalps his comrades had swinging in the breeze. A quick glance would tell you what your standing in the community was for that week or month. "Family connections" meant nothing as inheritance was taboo. You got a chieftancy via your own personal achievements. As a matter of fact, you didn't even inherit the family name. So the scalp, along with a stolen rifle or stolen horse, was concrete evidence of bravery and superiority over the enemy.

The scalp was removed under various conditions. Some tribes held that the scalp must be from an enemy or it would bring disgrace to the warrior. But, again, there were times when the enemy might include anyone. This was illustrated during the Revolutionary War when the enemy could either be a "red or blue coated scalp." It depended upon whether the source of reimbursement was the United States or Britain. For many tribes scalping was not an act or method of killing. Unknowingly or accidentally the Indian might take a scalp from an unconscious victim that had been mistaken for dead. There had been numerous living evidences of such happenings.

It is usually thought that scalping was a monopoly of the Indian, but white men were also guilty. The Mountain men of the 1830s in their lonely, dangerous trek for beaver skins had reverted to savagry and they took their share of scalps.

The method of taking the scalp was swift and bloody. The one-fourth inch scalp lies snugly over the bony skull and the only vital structures encountered are the abundant blood vessels in the scalp itself. One could readily bleed to death from such a blood loss, but at the same time a good bit of pressure applied to the area would stop the hemorrhage. There were such cases of survival and the only permanent damage was a cosmetic one. The brain is so well protected by its bony skull enclosure that scalping itself created no damage unless the head was struck by a heavy object to the extent that the skull would be fractured or the victim suffer from concussion.

The amount of scalp removed measured about the size of the palm of the hand or slightly larger. If the battle had subsided and the warrior had quickly ascertained that his own scalp was not in jeopardy, he would take additional hair. Any extra patches of hair meant that much more for scalp locks or other decorative purposes. The scalp had to contain the crown to be acceptable. That was the part from which the hair radiates from a central point.

It was of no consolation that the scalping was usually performed by a tool of civilized manufacture. The most widely used weapon was an ordinary cheap butcher knife. If one looked closely at the blade he would often see the initials G R. This stood for George Rex, an old stamp of British authenticity, and it was supposed to convince the Indian that he was getting the standard item. (It didn't take the trappers very long to change the meaning of the letters to Green River.) The British knife was single-bladed and heavy and, as such, it was much more used and liked than the lighter, double-bladed American knife. The heavy knife often had a blade whose back side was one-half inch thick. Sitting Bull's museum piece is an example of this. If the Indian got his knife in 1832 he probably traded his sixty-dollar horse to obtain the two dollar item.

The battle over, the war booty was brought home. The scalp was dried and it was then curiously ornamented and displayed as a trophy in many forms. The most common way of keeping a scalp was to stretch it on a small hoop and attach it to a long stick about two feet long. This was the form generally used in the scalp dance. Other smaller scalps or patches of hair were attached to different parts of clothing as in the form of fringes on the sleeves of garments. Still other trophies were suspended from the bridles of their horse and used in parades. The skin side of the scalp was often painted entirely red or one half red and one half black. The other hairy side was usually braided. Some scalps were suspended from a pole over the wigwam. This was the often-described "scalp-pole." The paintings of George Catlin in the National Museum at Washington, D.C., accurately portray the various scalp preparations.

Having served their ceremonial purpose, the scalps were disposed of in different ways.

In most cases, the scalp was treated with great respect while in use. Some tribes regarded the scalps with fear and had to purify them and pray over them to keep them harmless. Such was the case of the Papagos and Pina Indians of Arizona. It was this tribe which permitted only designated priest-like men to take the scalps. Often times the scalps were buried after a series of public exhibitions. The burial was accompanied by the mournful songs which were howled or sung for the benefit of the victims. Some tribes placed the scalps on buffalo chips and left them on the battleground as a sacrifice to the sun god. The Dakota tribe destroyed theirs after one year of use in order to release the enemy spirits from their earthly ties. Some scalps continued to adorn the warrior's clothing or his horse. Others were used in sacred medicine bundles.

The Indian and his scalping have long disappeared from the American scene and yet no one really knows just how much conscience these warriors actually harbored. This so-called stoic Indian certainly had a superstitious dread of the spirits of his slain enemies. Many have remarked about the noble eyes of the Indian which belied his savagery.

A war party of great daring would come home bearing fresh scalps. It was a triumphant return which called for a celebration—a scalp dance. Scalps both old and new were used. The women brought forth all the tribe's old scalps. It was in the scalp dance alone that women did lead a tribal ritual or don warrior's apparel. Lewis Garrad in his book *Wah-To-Yah* gives us one of the most authentic versions of the scalp dance. He had been invited by the chiefs of the Cheyenne tribe to join and watch the dance. On this particular occasion the scalps were from the Pawnee. He joined the chiefs as they sat down by a huge pile of fired dry logs. The dance was usually held at night and light was furnished by the large fire. The faces of the girls were either brilliant with vermillion or dark with a blackening soil mixture. The dress was covered with beads and porcupine quillwork. Their arms and fingers were covered with brass bracelets or rings. Shells of various kinds dangled from their ears. There were approximately two hundred women and two hundred and fifty men who joined together to form a huge circle and then moved around in a shuffling step. Inside this circle, and marching in a contrary direction, were twenty-five drummers and musicians. Surrounding this group were many hundreds of onlookers. There was the thud of the drums and the singing of the dancers. It started slowly, but the pace accelerated as the scalps of the slain were borne aloft. The scalps were shaken wildly for all to see—as battle pennants atop their tall poles. This affair often lasted for two or more days.

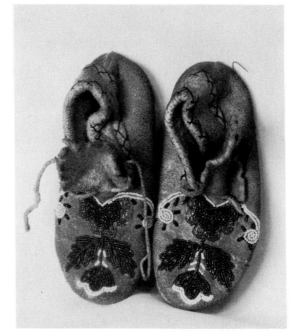

Sioux moccasins

51

Fears The Eagle—Oglala Sioux

Mummified Shoshone

Photo—Hillers, courtesy Smithsonian Inst.

Cheyenne Chief Starving Elk

Hunkpapa Sioux bride

Pretty Sea Shells—daughter of White Bull

Youth Was Not Served

Prior to the Beecher Island fight in 1868, eight young Indians acted on their own initiative to do some creditable act in order to win acclaim from the chiefs of the Sioux camp. Two of the young braves were Cheyenne—Starving Elk (photo opposite page) and Little Hawk—the rest Sioux.

The exact whereabouts of the white soldiers under Major Forsyth were unknown to the Indians and the youths set out to find them. During the night they rode from hill to hill, stopping frequently to listen with their ears to the ground. Just before daybreak they saw fires being kindled and as they rode quietly forward there was just enough light to show them a great number of horses and mules.

Impulsively, making all the noise they could, waving blankets and robes, they charged the herd to stampede it. A few horses broke loose but out of the whole mass, the young Indians caught only seven.

The thoughtless raid cost the Sioux far more than they gained by the acquisition of a few horses. It gave the white scouts alarm and the first knowledge that the Indians were aware of their nearness. Major Forsyth was able to entrench his command on Beecher Island and withstand the Sioux attack.

Lone Elk—Sioux

*Touch The Cloud
—Cheyenne*

*Chief Yellow Boy
—Sioux*

**Photos (opp. and top) Heyn & Matzen,
(right) Rinehart, courtesy Smithsonian
Inst.**

Waiting for signal to charge

Old time warrior is shown, bow and arrow in position, two extra shafts in the bow hand, another between the teeth for instant use.

Chapter Six

The FREEMANS
and the FRONTIER

I CAME FROM Canada to Leavenworth, Kansas. Mr. Freeman was a freighter to Pike's Peak, but was not always successful. He spent $4,000 on one train and came back with only a team of oxen and a team of ponies. The next spring, 1862, I bought a stage-coach and using the pony team, I took my three children, the youngest only two months old, and drove all the way to Nebraska. My husband was there and had started a little store just across from the pony express station on Plum Creek. He bought buffalo hides of the Indians and shipped them east. The buffalo were in easy reach and we had fresh meat every day. We had a big sign with the word "Bakery" on it. I baked a hundred pounds of flour every day. I would make yeast bread over night and would bake it in the fore-noon, and make salt-rising in the morning and bake it in the afternoon. We got St. Louis flour that the freighters brought from Denver when they came back. I sold my bread for fifty cents a loaf and made as much as thirty dollars a day. I made cheese, too. We had seventy-five head of cows and milked twenty-five. We would take a young calf and let it fill its stomach with its mother's milk, then kill it. Then we took the stomach and washed and wiped it and hung it up on a nail to dry. When it was perfectly dry we would put it away carefully in a cloth and used it for rennett to make the cheese. I would put in a little piece of it in new milk and it would form a solid curd. My husband made me a press and a mold. I got twenty-five cents a pound for my cheese, and sold lots of it. I got up fine meals and charged two dollars a meal. The people were glad to pay it. There was plenty of firewood. The trees drifted down the river and we piled the wood up on the islands, but after the settlers came they would steal it. There was no need of anybody going hungry those days, for anyone could kill a buffalo. One day a herd of thirty came within ten feet of our door, and our cows went away with them. The children and I walked three miles before we came up to the cows and could get them back home. We were near the river and it was not far down to water. We dug holes in the ground and sunk five salt barrels. The water came up in these and we always had plenty of water. Sometimes we dipped the barrels dry, but they would be full the next morning. There wasn't a pump in the country for years.

The people who kept the Pony Express station were named Humphries. These stations were about fifty miles apart. There would be lots of people at the station every night, for after the Indians became troublesome, the people went in trains of about a hundred wagons. There were many six oxen teams. The Indians never troubled any-body until the whites killed so many buffalo and wasted so much. There were carcas-ses all over the prairies. The Indians used every part, and they knew this great slaughter

This account titled "Recollections of the First Settler of Dawson County," by Mrs. Daniel Freeman, ap-peared in NEBRASKA REMINISCENCES, *Nebraska So-ciety of Daughters of the American Revolution.*

of the buffalo meant starvation for them, so they went on the warpath in self-defense. They would skulk on the river bank where the trail came close, and would rush up and attack the travelers. The soldiers were sent out as escorts and their families often went with them. One night at Plum Creek Pony Express station twin babies were born to the lieutenant and wife. I went over in the morning to see if I could help them, but they were all cared for by the lieutenant. He had washed the babies and had the tent in order. I do not remember his name now. We often saw tiny babies with their mothers lying in the wagons that came by. They would be wrapped up, and looked very comfortable. Water was so scarce that they had to pay for enough to wash the babies.

Brigham Young made trip after trip wiith foreign people of all kinds but blacks. Most of these could not speak English, and I don't think Brigham bought any water for them, as they were filthy dirty. Brigham was a great big fat man, and he kept himself pretty neat. He made just about one trip a year. One company of immigrants was walking through, and the train was a couple of miles long. They went south of the river on the Oregon trail. There was no other road then.

On August 8, 1864, the Sioux people killed eleven men at 11:00 o'clock in the morning, on Elm Creek. I was afraid to stay on our ranch, so I took the children and started to Fort Kearny. On our way we came to the place of the massacre. The dead men were lying side by side in a long trench, their faces were covered with blood and their boots were on. Three women were taken prisoners. I heard that there were two children in the party, and that they were thrown in the grass, but I looked all around for them and didn't find any signs of them. Friends of these people wrote to Mr. E. M. F. Leflang, to know if he could locate them. The Indians never troubled us except to take one team during this war, but I was always afraid when I saw the soldiers coming. They would come in the store and help themselves to tobacco, cookies, or anything. Then the teamsters would swing their long black-snake whips and bring them down across my chickens heads, then pick them up and carry them to camp. I think the officers were the most to blame for they sold the soldiers' rations, and the men were hungry.

When the Union Pacific railroad was first built we lived on our homestead north of the river and the town was started on our land. We had the contract to supply the wood for the engines. They didn't use any other fuel then. We hired men to cut the wood on Wood river where Eddyville and Sumner are now. I boarded the men in our new big house across from the depot in old Plum Creek. The store was below and there was an outside stairway for the men to go up. That summer Mr. Freeman was in Washington, Philadelphia, and New York talking up this country. Mr. Freeman was the first county clerk and his office was upstairs over the store. We rented some of the rooms to newcomers. We did a big business until the railroad moved the town to their section, a mile west. Mr. Freeman kept on trapping, and finally was drowned near Deadwood, South Dakota. I stayed by Dawson county and raised my family and they all are settled near me and have good homes.

Cheyenne Chief White Buffalo

Painting on buffalo skin

Photos (top) courtesy U. of Wyoming, (center) Jackson,
(right) Heyn & Matzen, courtesy Smithsonian Inst.

Chief Eagle Shirt—Sioux

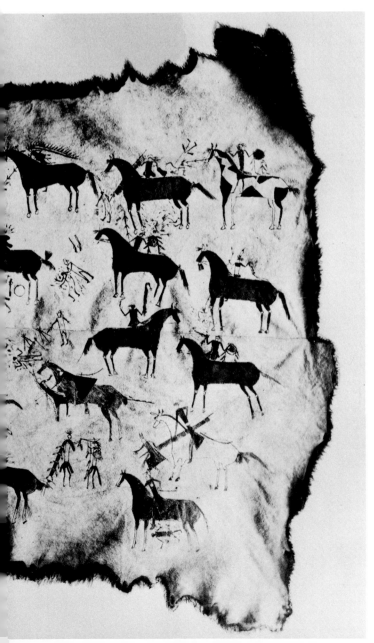

*Sioux group near
Ft. Laramie, 1868*

*Left to right: (standing) White Horse,
Black Foot, Yellow Bull, (sitting) Gray
Blanket,White Fawn, unnamed child,
Little Face, unnamed squaw.*

*Arapahoe Chief Powder
Face and squaw*

*Photos (top) Gardner, (left) Jackson,
courtesy Smithsonian Inst.*

Chapter Seven

AB-SA-RA-KA

THE CHEYENNES TALK

At twelve o'clock, June 16th, a few Indians appeared on the hills, and after showing a white flag and receiving assurance of welcome about forty, including the squaws of chiefs and warriors, approached the camp and bivouacked on the level ground in front. Meanwhile hospital tents had been arranged for this first interview with the inhabitants of Absaraka. A table covered with the national flag was placed across one tent, chairs were placed behind and at the ends for officers of the garrison, while other seats were placed in front for visitors.

Trunks were opened, epaulettes and dress hats were overhauled, so that whatever a full dress and a little ceremony could do by way of reaching the peculiar taste of the Indian for dignity and finery was done. The band of the 18th played without as the principal chiefs were brought across the parade-ground to the tents and introduced to their seats by Mr. Adair. The Cheyennes came in full state, with their best varieties of costume, ornament, and arms; though there was occasionally a departure from even the Indian originality in apparel. One very tall warrior, with richly wrought moccasins and a fancy breech-cloth, had no other covering for his person than a large gay umbrella, which as his pony galloped briskly up, had far more of the grotesque and ludicrous in its associations than it had of the warlike and fearful.

Some were bare to the waist, others had only the limbs bare. Some wore elaborate necklaces of grizzly bears' claws, shells, and continuous rings, bead-adorned moccasins, leggings, tobacco pouches, medicine bags, and knife scabbards, as well as armlets, earrings, and medals.

The larger silver medals included, one each, of the administrations and bore the medallion heads and names of Jefferson, Madison, and Jackson. These medals had evidently belonged to their fathers who had visited Washington, or had been the trophies of the field or trade.

Those who claimed pre-eminence among the land were "Black Horse," "Red Arm," "Little Moon," "Pretty Bear," "The Rabbit that Jumps," "The Wolf that Lies Down," "The Man that Stands alone on the Ground," and "Dull Knife."

As these were the Indians who had sent the message of the 14th, or were in their company, the question of their inclination and temper was one of no little interest to all.

The formal assurance of the Laramie Peace Commission before its adjournment, that satisfactory peace had been made with the Ogillalla and Brule Sioux, and that the Arapahoe and Cheyenne had only to come in for their presents, inspired some hope that possibly the reception of this first band encountered, might result in substantial advantage beyond the mere range of the band itself.

As the front of the canvas was open, the ladies gathered in the headquarters tent close by, parted its folds and enjoyed a dress-circle view of the whole performance. As pipes passed and the inevitable *"how,"* the rising up, and the shaking of hands were in-

From the book AB-SA-RA-KA. Home of the Crows: Being the Experience of an Officer's Wife on the Plains—*by Mrs. Margaret Irvin (Sullivant) Carrington.*

terludes between all solemn declarations, as well as the prelude to a new speech, or the approval of something good that had been said, the scene seemed just about as intelligible as a rapidly-acted pantomime would be to a perfect stranger to the stage.

The red-sandstone pipe had its frequent replenishing before a single "how" indicated that either visitor wished to make himself heard. The scene was peculiar.

In front of them all, and to the left of the table, sitting on a low seat, with elbows on his knees and chin buried in his hands, sat the noted James Bridger, whose forty-four years upon the frontier had made him as keen and suspicious of Indians as any Indian himself could be of another. The old man, already somewhat bowed by age, after long residence among the Crows as a friend and favorite chief, and having incurred the bitter hatred of the Cheyennes and Sioux alike, knew full well that *his* scalp ("Big Throat's") would be the proudest trophy they could bear to their solemn feasts; and there he sat, or crouched, as watchful as though old times had come again, and he was once more to mingle in the fight, or renew the ordeal of his many hair-breadth escapes and spirited adventures. Many stories are told of his past history, and he is charged with many of his own manufacture. He is said to have seen a diamond in the Rocky Mountains, by the light of which he traveled thirty miles one stormy night, and to have informed some inquisitive travelers that Scott's Bluff, nearly four hundred feet high, now stands where there was a deep valley when he first visited the country. When inquired of as to these statements, he quietly intimated that there was no harm in fooling people who pumped him for information and would not even say *"thank ye."* Once he was wealthy, and his silver operations in Colorado might have been very lucrative; but he was the victim of misplaced confidence, and was always restless when not on the plains. To us, he was invariably straightforward, truthful, and reliable. His sagacity, knowledge of woodcraft, and knowledge of the Indian was wonderful, and his heart was warm and his feelings tender wherever he confided or made a friend. An instance of this will close the sketch of one who will soon pass away, the last of the first pioneers of the Rocky Mountains.

He cannot read, but enjoys reading. He was charmed by Shakespeare; but doubted the Bible story of Samson's tying foxes by the tails, and with firebrands burning the wheat of the Philistines. At last he sent for a good copy of Shakespeare's plays, and would hear them read until midnight with unfeigned pleasure. The murder of the two princes in the Tower startled him to indignation. He desired it to be read a second and a third time. Upon positive conviction that the text was properly read to him, he burned the whole set, convinced that "Shakespeare must have had a bad heart and been as de—h mean as a Sioux, to have written such scoundrelism as that." But to return to the council.

Near Major Bridger stood Jack Stead, the interpreter. Born in England, early a runaway sailor boy, afterward a seaman upon the *Peacock* when it was wrecked near the mouth of the Columbia River; then traversing the Rocky Mountains as one of the first messengers to report the Mormon preparations to resist the United States, and the renewal of Indian hostilities, the same year; with hair and eyes black as an Indian's, and a face nearly as tawny from hardship and exposure; a good shot, and skilled in woodcraft; with a Cheyenne wife; fond of big stories and much whisky; but a fair interpreter when mastered and held to duty; and watchful as Bridger himself to take care of his scalp—Jack Stead was the first to break the silence and announce that Black Horse wanted to talk.

Adjutant Phisterer, called by the Indians "Roman, or Crooked Nose," acted as recorder of the council, keeping full notes of the conference; and few were the diaries or letters home that did not embody the history of our first visit from Indians, and repeat some of their expressions of purpose or desire.

Neither did the Indian advocate appear to disadvantage, as the exponent of his rights and wants. Erect and earnest, he cast off the buffalo robe that had been gathered about his shoulders and in his folded arms, and while it now hung loosely from his girdle, stepped halfway toward the table and began.

With fire in his eye, and such spirit in his gesture as if he were striking a blow for his life or the life of his nation; with cadence changeful, now rising in tone, so as to sound far and wide over the garrison, and again sinking so as to seem as if he were communing with his own spirit rather than feeling for a response from the mind of another, the Cheyenne chief stood there to represent his people, to question the plans of the white chief, and solemnly advise him of the issue that was forced upon the red man. It was an occasion when all idea of the red man as the mere wild beast to be slaughtered, quickly vanished in a prompt sympathy with his condition, and no less inspired an earnest purpose, so far as possible, to harmonize the intrusion upon his grand hunting domain with his best possible well-being in the future.

Other chiefs followed "Black Horse," in harangues of varied length and vigor; and all agreed that they preferred to accept protection and become the friends of the whites. They came to represent one hundred and seventy-six lodges, and had been hunting on Goose Creek and Tongue River, when they met Red Cloud; but said that one hundred and twenty-five of their young men were absent with "Bob Tail," having gone to the Arkansas on the war-path and hunt. They had quarreled with another band of Cheyennes, who lived near the Black Hills east of Powder River; and said there was a third band south of the Republican hostile to the whites. Two of the chiefs had with them Comanche wives whom they had married in excursions to the south.

They gave the history of a portion of our march, and stated correctly, what Red Cloud had assured them, that half of the white soldiers were left back at Crazy Woman's Fork. They said that Red Cloud told them, the morning before the messenger was sent to the camp, that white soldiers from Laramie would be at Piney Fork before the sun was overhead in the heavens; that the white chief sent soldiers from Reno after Indians who stole horses and mules; but the white soldiers did not get them back.

They also stated that the Sioux were having a sun-dance, insisting that the Cheyennes must make common cause with them and drive the white man back to Powder River; that some of Red Cloud's men had already gone back to interrupt travel on the road; that they had left their squaws in the village with thirty of their old men, and were afraid the Sioux would rob them in their absence if they should stay too long in the white man's camp; but that if they could have provisions, they would make a strong peace, and let a hundred of their young men, whose return would be in two days, go with the white soldiers against the Sioux.

Before the council broke up, Brevet Major Haymond arrived with his four companies and went into camp northwest of the fort near the river crossing.

The Indians became very restless as the afternoon progressed, and at last bade good-by; receiving papers indicative of their good behavior, and entering into an agreement to leave the line of road and go up on or south of the upper plateau of the Big Horn Mountains. They afterward visited Fort Caspar, behaving well, and no doubt observed their obligations as best they could.

The presents given consisted of some second hand clothing of the officers, twenty pounds of tobacco, a dinner of army rations, and enough flour, bacon, sugar and coffee to give them a meal in their village and convince the absent of their kind treatment. They left with apparently cordial good feeling, and the understanding that they were not to approach emigrant trains even to beg; but might go to Laramie, or other military posts when hungry, as long as they remained the friends of the whites.

There is no evidence that any of these chiefs have violated their pledges.

THE SIOUX ATTACK

At five o'clock a.m., July 17th, the herds of Brevet Major Haymond were surprised, the Indians crawling within the picket, and with great sagacity starting Wagonmaster Hill's bell mare first, so as to secure all in company. Major Haymond, with one orderly, started in pursuit, as we afterward learned, although no information was given at the post until two hours after. He left orders, we heard, for the mounted men to saddle and follow. The party thus pursuing in haste was ultimately surrounded by several hundred Indians, and when a messenger was sent in with report of the condition of affairs, two companies of infantry and fifty mounted men, with ammunition, rations, wagons, and ambulances, were at once started to the relief.

But very soon sad reports came from Peno valley, only a few miles over Lodge Trail Ridge. The casualties of the command had been two men killed and three wounded; and, more painful than all, was the report of the massacre on the road of Louis Gazzons and most of his party.

Brevet Major Haymond, finding the Indians so numerous and the ground impracticable for the use of his men, while the Indians were not only perfectly at home, but specifically watchful of stragglers and fully versed in that style of warfare, fell back toward the post. On the retreat he came up with the wagons of French Pete, which had already started for camp. About the plundered wagons lay the mutilated remains of his party, with the exception that his wife, a Sioux woman, with her five children, had been able to hide in the brush until the arrival of troops as an escort to headquarters.

Six men lay dead and mutilated upon the road. Such was the first lesson to the expedition of the kind of peace to be expected in the future. Henry Arrison, of St. Louis, partner of Gazzons, was among the number. The cattle, wagons, and goods that the Indians had not broken open, for want of time, were brought to the post and taken charge of by Mr. John W. Hugus, administrator, on behalf of the widow, creditors, and friends.

The Sioux wife of Gazzons said that the Cheyennes had tradely largely and pleasantly with Pete, and that the chiefs who had visited the post on the 16th were with them until midnight, smoking and trading; that during the evening some of the Sioux chiefs came up from Tongue River valley and asked Black Horse what the white man said to them, and whether the white chief was going back to Powder River. To this Black Horse answered "that the white chief would not go back, but his soldiers would go out." They then asked "what presents were given." Black Horse told them "that they had all they wanted to eat, and the white chief wished all the Arapahoes and Sioux, and all other Indians of that country, to go to Laramie and sign the treaty and get their presents." At this the Sioux unstrung their bows, and whipped Black Horse and the other Cheyennes over the back and face, crying "Coo!" which by the Indians is deemed a matter of prowess and a feat which secures them credit, as they count their "Coos" in a fight almost as proudly as they do the scalps of enemies.

After the Sioux left, Black Horse told French Pete that he must go to his village and from there to the mountains, for the Sioux meant war, but advised *him* to send a messenger to the white chief quick, or the Sioux would kill him. French Pete neglected the advice; but was on his return in the morning, when the Sioux, who had stolen Major Haymond's mules, and had come in contact with his men, came across the train and destroyed all the men who were with it.

On the same day Major Haymond's four companies were ordered to change their position and encamp below the fort.

On the 19th a train with military escort, under Captain Burrows, was sent back to Fort Reno for provisions. The young men of the Cheyennes also returned from the Arkansas, and "Bob Tail" had an interview with the colonel, leaving his own robe as a pledge of his friendship.

About one o'clock A.M., July 24th, a runner from Clear Fork brought a dispatch from Captain Burrows that the Sioux were very numerous, and additional force was needed at once. Mr. Thomas Dillon also wrote that Mr. Kirkendall's train had been engaged all the afternoon, and he could not move without troops. A company of infantry, with a mountain howitzer soon started, and upon their approach in the morning, the Indians, numbering several hundred, fled. Torrence Callery, of Company C, had been killed; and one of the trains relieved, which had been taken back to Fort Reno temporarily, contained five officers of the regiment with servants, baggage, Mrs. Lieutenant Ware and child, all of whom had been forwarded from Fort Laramie, under the prestige of the treaty, with only ten men as escort to headquarters. When this train had reached Crazy Woman's Fork it was attacked by fifty Indians, and Lieutenant Daniels, of Indiana, who was a little in advance selecting camping ground was killed, scalped, and mutilated, while one of the Indians put on his clothes and danced within view of the party.

Chaplain David White, Lieutenants Templeton, Bradley, and Wands, with Mrs. Wands and child, survived, and the Henry rifle of Mr. Wands was specially efficacious in warding off and punishing the assailants.

Chaplain White, like the preachers of Cromwell, only prayed *internally*, while putting his time physically into the best exercise of self-defense. He thinks he did his duty; and the officers say that he thought it was just about the right thing to kill as many of the varmint as possible.

Lieutenant Kirtland's rescuing party from Reno was also very prompt, and Lieutenant Daniel's remains were escorted to the post and suitably buried.

The Cheyennes of Black Horse met Kirkendall's train and gave warning of the approach of the Sioux, just as they had at the council given indications of this same movement. The warning was disregarded, but the Sioux *did* come.

Thus commenced our first two weeks in our new home. A few more incidents will illustrate the experience that followed.

July 22d. At Buffalo Springs, on the Dry Fork of Powder River, a citizen train was attacked, having one man killed and another wounded.

July 22d. Indians appeared at Fort Reno, driving off one public mule.

July 22d. Mr. Nye lost four animals near Fort Phil Kearney, and Mr. Axe and Mr. Dixon each had two mules stolen by Indians.

July 23d. A citizen train was attacked at the Dry Fork of the Cheyenne, and two men were killed.

July 23d. Louis Cheney's train was attacked; one man was killed, and horses, cattle, and private property were sacrificed.

July 28th. Indians attempted to drive off the public stock at Fort Reno, and failed; but took the cattle of citizen John B. Sloss. Pursuit; recovered them.

July 29th. A citizen train was attacked at Brown Springs, four miles east of the East Fork of the Cheyenne, and eight men were killed, two were wounded, and one of those died of his wounds. Their grave is still memorial of the confidence with which they left Laramie, assured that all was peace. These men, though too few in numbers, were well armed, but were deceived by a show of friendship; and one Indian shot a white man in the back just after shaking hands and receiving a present.

Meanwhile, the necessity of maintaining Fort Reno as an intermediate post on the route had been established. Another company was sent to reinforce its garrison. The Upper Yellowstone post was abandoned for want of troops, and early in August, Brevet Lieutenant-Colonel N. C. Kinney, with Captain Burrows and their two companies, were sent to the Big Horn River, distant ninety-one miles, to establish that post, subsequently known as Fort C. F. Smith.

The narrative of *all* hostile demonstrations need not be traced. Enough will be given to correct false ideas as to the feelings and operations of Indians during the year; and the reader will not be astonished that ladies, as well as gentlemen, perused the President's message of December 8th, 1866, which congratulated the country that the Indians were at peace, with something like inquisitiveness as to whether the colonel had reported the true condition to department headquarters, and whether department headquarters had read his report.

But to proceed. Grover, the artist, correspondent of Frank Leslie, was scalped one Sunday morning, while only a few minutes' walk from the post.

September 8th, at 6 o'clock A.M. Twenty mules were driven from a citizen herd, during a severe storm, within a mile of Fort Phil Kearney; and two other demonstrations were made the same day. The colonel with one party, and Lieutenant Adair with another, were out until after 9 o'clock at night in pursuit.

September 10th. Ten herders were attacked a mile south of the fort, losing twenty-three horses and seventy-eight mules. Pursuit was vigorous, but unsuccessful.

September 13th. At midnight a summons came from the hay contractors, Messrs. Crary and Carter, at Goose Creek, for help, as one man had been killed, hay had been heaped upon five mowing-machines and set on fire, and two hundred and nine cattle had been stolen by the Indians, who had driven a herd of buffalo into the valley, and thus taken buffalo and cattle together out of reach.

Lieutenant Adair went at once with reinforcements, but found the Indians in too large force for continuance of the work.

September 23d. Indians attacked and drove off twenty-four head of cattle. They were pursued by Quartermaster Brown, in company with twenty-three soldiers and citizens, and after a sharp fight at close quarters, the cattle were recaptured, and a loss was inflicted upon the Indians of thirteen killed and many wounded.

September 23d. Lieutenant Matson, with an escort, bringing wagons from the hay field, was surrounded and corraled for some time by a superior force. He found upon the road the body of contractor Grull, who had been to Fort C. F. Smith with public stores, and was killed on his return with two of his drivers.

On the 17th, 21st, and 23d, Indians had also been active near Fort Reno, driving off horses and cattle. Casper H. Walsh was killed; and at the Dry Fork of the Cheyenne, citizens W. R. Pettis and A. G. Overholt were wounded.

September 27th. Private Patrick Smith was scalped at the Pinery, but crawled a half mile to the block-house, and survived twenty-four hours.

Two of the working party in the woods were also cut off from their comrades by nearly one hundred Indians, and were scalped before their eyes. A party of fifteen dashed at the nearest picket but did no harm.

Captain Bailey's mining party lost two of their best men.

On one occasion a messenger came in hot haste from the Pinery, reporting that they were besieged; that the Indians had fired through the loop-holes of the block-house; that the men were constantly under arms, unwilling as well as unable to work, and asking for a force to clear the Indians out of the bottom lands underneath, where the woods were very dense. The colonel went out with a small party and howitzer, shelled the woods, restored confidence, and the men resumed work. A person ignorant of the effect of a case shot, which scatters its eighty iron bullets quite dangerously, might think it very foolish to explode one where no enemy was *in sight*: but we saw those experiments repeated, where otherwise quite a skirmishing party would have been required, and as the Indians invariably ran away, and sometimes got hurt, the little howitzers were soon favorites and no objects of ridicule or contempt.

The foregoing are instances out of many Indian visits, but do not give all, even of the first two months of our residence in that country. Alarms were constant; attacks upon the trains were frequent, and this kind of visitation continued during the whole season. The ladies all came to the conclusion, no less than the officers affirmed it, that the Laramie treaty was *"Wau-nee-chee,"* NO GOOD!

THE ARROW BEATS THE REVOLVER

Popular opinion has regarded the Indian bow and arrow as something primitve and well enough for the pursuit of game, but quite useless in a contest with the white man. This idea would be excellent if the Indian warriors would calmly march up in line of battle and risk their masses so armed against others armed with the rifle. But the Indian comes as the hornet comes, in clouds or singly, yet never trying to sting until his ascendency is assured and his own exposure is slight.

At fifty yards a well-shapen, iron-pointed arrow is dangerous and very sure. A handful drawn from the quiver and discharged successively will make a more rapid fire than that of the revolver, and at very short range will farther penetrate a piece of plank or timber than the ball of an ordinary Colt's navy pistol.

The arrow-head varies in length and shape, and the shaft itself slightly changes, according to the tastes of different bands or tribes; and yet so constantly are arrows exchanged in gambling or barter that the character of the arrow used does not invariably determine the tribe engaged. Such were many of the arrows taken from the bodies of Captains Fetterman, Brown, Lieutenant Grummond, and others, after the massacre of December, 1866. All the peculiarities there found have been seen in the quivers of the Kittekehas, Chowees, Petropowetaws, and other Pawnees, all of whom are friendly, and some of whom are now, as in the winter of 1865-6, in the employ of the United States. The head is often barbed, but not generally, and is from two to three and a half inches in length, made of iron, and ground to a double edge. The shaft, which is about twenty-five inches in length, is winged by three feathers of the eagle, sage-hen, or wild goose, and from the sinew wrapping of the head to that which binds the feathers is deeply marked by three grooves or blood-seams, so that when the flesh of man or beast closes about the shaft, these seams act as conduits and gradually bleed the victim to death. These grooves are with some Indians straight, and with others are zigzag or winding from midway down to the feathers.

The bows of Ogillalla and Brule Sioux, Arapahoes, Cheyennes, and most of the Indians east of the Rocky Mountains, are from thirty-two to forty inches long, of great elasticity and tension, so that they easily drive an arrow through a two-inch plank, and even through a man or buffalo.

The hatchet is generally that which is furnished by Indian agents or traders, often having the head and handle hollow and connected for use as a pipe; and, when possible, the handle itself is profusely studded with brass nails such as once distinguished parlor sofas and chairs.

Rifles, both English and American, abound. The "Hawkins" is a favorite, carrying what is called the "trade ball," and requiring a patch; but many of the old guides, trappers, and halfbreeds still cling to their use as in the days of Pathfinder and other heroes of Cooper.

The quiver and bow-case are made of deerskin, bearskin, otter and other hides, or furs; and the armament of Hawkeye, which now hangs before the writer, is elaborate with tassels and pendants from well-dressed beaver.

The shield is worn by many of the leading braves, and is formed of several thicknesses of hide fastened through and through about the edge with sinew, and studded with brass nails, or ornamented with silver and other bright metal.

The spear varies from five and a half to seven feet in length, having a head nearly eighteen inches long, with a small pennon; and the heel of the shaft is balanced with eagle feathers, while others are caught along the shaft, giving steadiness to the flight, and suiting the diversified tastes of the owner.

The right and left hair of the warrior or brave is brought before the ear, braided or twisted, and wrapped with strings or ribbons, and falling upon the breast; while a third braid, falling behind and below the scalp-lock or tuft, often is covered with a succession of silver medallions hammered from coin, gradually diminishing in size from four inches to one inch as the series approaches the ground.

Earrings, necklaces, bracelets, and armlets are of brass, beads, bears' claws, or silver, but more generally of beautiful combinations of shells from the Pacific, seventy-five of which have been the price of a pony, and show the close relations of trade maintained between the tribes of the opposite slopes of the Rocky Mountains.

Moccasins, leggings, breech-cloth, and a buffalo robe belted about the waist, leaving the breast bare, is the sole dress of the majority. Others have jackets more or less fancifully decorated with small bullet buttons, and every article of dress that an American soldier uses is at once assumed when its possession is acquired. Trousers are, however, cut off at the hip, as their own style of protection is habitually preferred. Gifts of clothing are quickly put on; and a present of gentlemen's underclothes once given to a Pawnee was so quickly substituted for his original garments as barely to allow escape from the room during the process.

The women vary little in costume except in a wrapping something like a petticoat or skirt, but wear less paint. The hair-parting is, however, invariably painted vermillion when visiting or in full dress, and cheeks, chin, and arms have their share of brilliant tints. Warriors, squaws, and children alike use the bow and arrow, but the women are peculiarly apt with knife and hatchet. The youngsters have a javelin exercise which is admirably fitted to prepare them for their future life. A small hoop is held by the thumb and forefinger of the right hand, while within the hand is the spear. The hoop is thrown forward on the ground, and the javelin is sent after and through the ring with great dexterity and success. This, with the cast of the hatchet and play of the knife, takes the place of the white boy's baseball or marbles; and the blunt-headed arrow brings down birds and small game that would be spoiled by the keener shaft.

The revolver is becoming quite common, and is used with more dexterity and skill than is the rifle. The following instance will illustrate a remarkable failure in rifle firing. Soon after Captain Fetterman arrived, he rode to the Pinery with Lieutenant Bisbee, Captain Ten Eyck, and one or two other officers who had just arrived, to see the locality. They descended to Pine Island just after the last timber-wagon had come out on the road, and in advance of their escort. They were received by a volley of from fifteen to twenty rifle shots, which were fired from a rest upon a fallen tree, at a distance of only fifty paces, as actually measured, without injury to anybody. A second volley equally failed to touch a man. A little bugle-boy brought word to the garrison that all were killed, for he saw the Indians as they fired and the officers as they disappeared. They were compelled to skirmish down the island before they could extricate themselves from the dilemma. A supporting party went out, but met them returning, and thus relieved the anxiety of the garrison.

The Indians not only use mirrors and flags for signal purposes, but many carry with them good field and spy-glasses, some of English styles, procured from Canada, and others are supplied by traders on the frontier.

The domestic life of the Indian, with the barbarity of the sun-dance and the filth of his home, have been often described; but the plentitude of furs in the land of Absaraka have furnished peculiar facilities for adornment and somewhat better wardrobes than are usual nearer the Lower Missouri and Mississippi waters. Their tepah (tepee, or lodge) is the model from which the Sibley tent was derived, and will accommodate several families; but nothing else on the face of the earth will furnish a more curious medley of contents than does a tepah where two or three families, of all ages and sizes, with all their worldly goods and hopes are huddled, piled, and crammed about its fire, and where the fitful wind and lazy squaws are combined in the effort to smoke buffalo tongues, strips of meat, and *Injun* all together. The picture is complete, by way of contrast, if a kettle of boiling water over the fire has received a fat dog just after his throat felt the knife, and a white officer, on a pile of furs, is doing his best to show how gracefully he can endure the honors and dinner specially designed for his presence. All this, too, while other officers and ladies are cheerfully waiting outside, glad to escape from the hospitality of a chief.

Bells, triangles, and common horns have found their way among these Indians, and they eagerly adopt from the white man whatever makes noise or show.

THE CROWS DECLARE FOR PEACE

It was quite early after the establishment of Fort Philip Kearney that measures were taken to hold communication with the Crow Indians, to consult with the authorities of

Montana, and determine the condition of the entire route to Virginia City. Major Bridger was selected for the mission, accompanied by Henry Williams, assistant guide, who proved himself valuable in almost every work he undertook. They made the through trip with comparative expedition, made complete notes of the journey, and besides their official reports, were very courteous in contributing their information to those who were desirous to keep a full record of all that transpired during our sojourn on the frontier.

They had first an interview with nearly six hundred warriors, not far from Clark's Fork. On that occasion "White Mouth," "Black Foot," and "Rotten Tail" declared their uniform and unanimous voice for peace; but said that in some instances the young men desired to join the Sioux, and thus come to some accommodation as to their title to the lands of which they had been robbed by both Sioux and Cheyennes.

Red Cloud had made them a visit and they had returned the visit, but would not join him against the whites. The "Man afraid of his Horses" told them that his young men were going on the war-path, and that the Sissetons, Bad Faces, Ogillallas from the Missouri, the Minneconjons from the Black Hills, the Unkpapas, some Cheyennes and Arapahoes, as well as the Gros Ventres of the Prairie, were united to drive away the whites, and would have big fights at the two new forts in the fall.

They also represented that "Iron Shell," with some of the young men of the Minneconjons and Brules, would go with Red Cloud, notwithstanding the Laramie treaty; that the Nesperces and Flatheads were friendly, but the Pagans and Bloods were hostile, while the Blackfeet, Assiniboines, and Crees were friendly with both parties and would join no league against the whites.

Besides the visits of Bridger to other bands of Crows along the route from Big Horn to the Upper Yellowstone, James Beckwith, the famous mulatto of the plains, who had also lived among the Crows as an adopted chief, and had several Crow wives, was employed as an assistant guide, and was sent to their villages, where he subsequently sickened and died.

From these sources it was learned that in the fight of September 23d the Sioux lost thirteen killed and had a great many wounded.

Other parties of Crows came to Fort C. F. Smith to hunt and trade in that vicinity, and not only showed uniform friendliness toward the whites and the new road, but offered two hundred and fifty young warriors to engage in operations against the Sioux. Major Bridger had great confidence in this proposition; but the officers had, it would seem, no authority to employ so many, as well as no means of arming and equipping them.

All the statements of the Crows were substantially confirmed by Cheyennes at a subsequent visit. They represented "Red Cloud" and "The Man afraid of his Horses" to be in Tongue River valley, and "Buffalo Tongue," to be on Powder River; that the "Big Bellies," the "Bad Arrows," "Those that wear a Bone in the Nose," and "Those that put Meat in the Pot" were near the Big Horn River, and though friendly to the Crows were opposed to the road; that "Bob North," a white man with but one thumb, with twenty-five lodges and the "Big Medicine Man of the Arapahoes," had also joined the aggressive party.

Still later in the season there was renewed and cumulative evidence that the Crows were truly friendly, but were unwilling to venture very far eastward for any purpose, until the Sioux were out of the way or the white soldiers were sufficiently numerous to guarantee their safety without sacrifice of life or property.

"White Mouth" and "Rotten Tail" told Mr. Bridger that they were half a day in riding through the hostile villages in Tongue River valley, and that fifteen hundred lodges of war parties were preparing to attack the white man at Fort Philip Kearney and Fort C. F. Smith.

All these statements were believed, and it is known that they had important influence in that vigorous prosecution of necessary work which followed, and rendered impossible any system of aggressive war on the part of the troops of the garrison.

THE INDIAN FIGHTS AGAINST FATE

When even a woman shares the contingencies of entering a new country with troops, she must learn something besides the lessons of housewifery, endurance, and patience.

When days, weeks, and months pass with constantly recurring opportunities of seeing Indians in small and in large parties dashing at pickets, driving in wood parties, harassing water details, and, with dancing and yelling, challenging the garrison to pursuit; when, now and then, one, two, or more casualties mark the issues of a day, and these culminate, until at least five wagonloads of bodies give evidence of the cunning barbarity and numbers of the foe; when night alarms are common, and three men are shot within thirty yards of the gates; when the stockade becomes a prison-wall, and over its trunks are seen only the signs of precaution or active warfare; when the men are never idle, but all are daily engrossed in essential labor, with no signs of reinforcement or aid; when the usual thankless task of opening a new country with its uncertainties and enmities, with resources absurdly deficient, meets only obloquy and abuse for the principal actors, she acquires *somehow,* whether by instinct or observation, it matters not which, an idea that Indians *will fight,* and sometimes do become quite wicked and dangerous. Surely, their ways are not as our ways, and their ponies are not like our horses. Their commissariat and their forage are not in trains or on pack mules; their campaigns are not extensively advertised in advance, nor do they move by regular stages or established routes.

Yes, even a woman, after several hundred miles of journey alternately in the ambulance or side saddle, sometimes in corral expecting its aid for safety, and again in the winding defile, where the very place excites the keenest scrutiny and is suggestive of noble red men with the nobility ignored, will see some peculiarities of Indian warfare when Indians are really venomous, and will draw conclusions for friends to consider, even if they only elicit a smile at her timidity, simplicity, or weakness.

James, the novelist, never compelled his solitary horseman to fight a Sioux, and, had the Knight of the Leopard, at the Diamond of the Desert, met more than one quiver of the darts of the Saracen, his adventures might have ended while his career was scarcely begun. Not unlike the Arab is the Indian of the Northwest. Isolated, yet in communication through the little mirrors which flash the sunlight and pass his signals for miles; separated, yet by the lance, pennon, and flags combined, when opportunity is inviting; dashing directly forward at a run, with the person crouched on the pony's neck, and wheeling only to throw himself out of sight and pass his arrows and bullets under the animal's neck before he returns for a fresh venture; fleeing everywhere, apparently at random, so that his pursuer must take choice of object of quest only to find his hot pursuit fruitless, with gathered numbers in his line of retreat; shooting up and down red buttes, where the horse of the white man breaks down at once; running on foot, with the trotting pony just behind him seeking a rest from the burden of his master; imitating the cry of the wolf and the hoot of the owl, when it will hide his night visit,—these Indians are everywhere, where you suppose they are not; and are certain not to be where you suppose them to be.

In ambush and decoy, *splendid;* in horsemanship, *perfect;* in strategy, *cunning;* in battle, *wary* and careful of life; in victory, jubilant; and in vengeance, fiendish and terrible.

Too few to waste life fruitlessly; too superstitious to leave their dead to the enemy; too cunning or niggardly of resources to offer fair fight; too fond of their choice hunting-grounds to yield willing possession to the stranger,—they wait and watch, and watch and wait, to gather the scalps of the unwary and ignorant, and bear off their trophies to new feasts, new orgies, and new endeavor.

So reluctant are they to attack a foe under cover, that during the year 1866—once before stated—not a train was lost or seriously embarrassed when in corral; nor was any considerable party assailed when it sought judicious and substantial defense. Yet, daring and watchful, none better estimate the foe they contend with. When white men have delivered their fire, and the gleam of the ramrod has shown that the single-shooting arm was in use, then follows the wild dash, with revolvers and arrows, so quick and so spirited that their loss is as nothing, and swift ponies take them safely away for renewal of attack. Circling and intermingling to confuse all aim, affecting retreat seemingly to break up their array, and by some ravine, gulch, canyon, or thicket to appear on fresh and better vantage-ground, they approximate ubiquity, and fill the terse description of the veteran Bridger, "Where there ain't no Injuns, you'll find 'em the thickest."

Good judges of numbers, and quick to estimate the strength and designs of an enemy; keen to maintain their scouts and secure due notice of reinforcements; rarely, though sometimes, fighting in masses, but then with such involved and concerted disorder as to insure their purpose, when the plan is to overwhelm alive and capture for the torture,—this same Indian must find in his final master a better-armed and well-disciplined foe, who has studied his country and his nature, and this before his peace-offerings will be abiding and honest, or his hunting-grounds shall become the peaceful path of the traveler.

With all this, these same Indians have read the book of fate, and in the establishment of mutually supporting and well-garrisoned strongholds they will be foiled as to protracted interruption of emigration and travel. When this end is reached, and the great route through Absaraka is occupied and guarded, the game will flee the range of the white man's rifle, and the desperate Indian must abandon his home, fight himself to death, or yield to the white man's mercy.

Fired by the progress of the settler and the soldier; seeing as never before the last retreat of the buffalo, the elk, and the deer invaded by a permanent intruder; looking at his rights as violated, and the promises of many agents as unfulfilled; taught by nature, if not by the white man, that he is the lawful tenant of the waste he roams over until he has bartered his right away,—he has some reason to exclaim, as Red Cloud assured Black Horse, when the latter, in July, 1866, said, "Let us take the white man's hand and what he gives us, rather than fight him longer and lose all,"—the answer was: "White man lies and steals. My lodges were many, but now they are few. The white man wants *all*. The white man must fight, and the Indian will die where his fathers died."

Growing conscious of the white man's power, knowing how vain is an open field struggle, they avoid such determining issues, and waylay in detail, gradually enlarging their sphere of action, and thereby gathering in the young men and disaffected of other bands, until common cause may be had of all whose wrongs or temper inspire them to keep the war-path longer.

The frequent change of dwelling-place in a great area of hunting-ground gives them peculiar aptitude for this warfare and peculiar immunity from punishment. A single pony will bear and drag the lodge poles of a tepah, and the squaws will not only relieve the warriors of all menial details, but with the old men and boys are no despicable protectors of a village when the fighting men are in pursuit of game or scalps.

Thus Indian fighting is no parade of ceremony specifically described in regulations, nor an issue between fair and generous opponents. It is at all times destruction for the white man to fail, and his exposures, his perils, and even his successes, so much less heralded and estimated than in more artificial war with those of his own race, only bring him the personal consciousness of duty done to balance wasting years, loss of social life, and a bare support. With all this, and the sometimes recurring feeling of bitterness prompting the desire to exterminate his foe and thereby visit upon him some of the horrid scenes he has passed through, there comes the inevitable sentiment of pity, and even of sympathy with the bold warrior in his great struggle; and in a dash over the plains, or breathing the pure air of the mountains, the sense of freedom and independence brings such contrast with the machinery and formalities of much that is called civilized life, that it seems but natural that the red man in his pride and strength should bear aloft the spear-point, and with new resolve fight the way through to his final home in the Spirit land.

Sioux near Ft. Laramie, 1868.

Left to right: Fox Tail, unnamed squaw, Yellow Bull, Yellow Top, Bull That Goes Hunting, Yellow Coat, Squaw Who Walks On Ice.

Arapahoe Chief Plenty Bears (left) and Old Eagle

Sioux Chief Crazy Bear

Photos (opp.) Heyn & Matzen, (top) Gardner, (right) Jackson, courtesy Smithsonian Inst.

"And the women waited for word from the battle"

Chiefs Crazy Bull and Friday—Arapahoe

Chief Painted Horse—Sioux

Photos (opp.) Heyn & Matzen, (right) Jackson,
courtesy Smithsonion Inst.,
(top) Nebraska State Hist. Soc.

Chapter Eight

INDIAN NOTES on the CUSTER BATTLE

O<small>N THE</small> T<small>ENTH</small> Anniversary of the Custer Battle held on the battlefield, June 25, 1886, many of the Indians who participated in the battle were present including Gall, Two Moons, White Bull, Crow King, and others. The soldiers who participated in these proceedings were all participants also in the Reno and Benteen engagement and knew as much about Custer's Last Stand as any white ever did or could know. These men were: General E. S. Godfrey, General Benteen, Captain McDougall, Capt. Edgerly, Dr. Porter, Colonel Partello, Colonel Slocum, and David F. Barry, famous Indian photographer.

Curley, the Crow scout who survived the battle, was also present. In the presence of all these witnesses, Chief Gall told and pantomimed the awful story of Custer's Last Stand.

"Gall talked slow and distinct," said Barry, "and the interpreter told us in short sentences what Gall had just said. None of those present disputed what Gall had said."

Gall first looked at Curley and said, "You have stated you were in this battle and that you got away. You were a coward and ran away before the battle began; if you hadn't, you would not be here today." Curley made no reply.

Standing besides the graves of Custer's Command, Gall continued, "It took about thirty-five minutes to wipe out this bunch of soldiers (Custer's), and I never saw men fight harder. They were right down on their knees firing and loading until the last man fell. I never saw any soldier offer to surrender. The smoke and dust was so thick that we could not always see the soldiers. The soldiers were fighting on foot, so finally we rode over them with our ponies. Our ponies were well-rested and fast runners, but the soldiers' horses were tired out before the battle began, and would not have been any good if the soldiers had been mounted. These soldiers were so hungry that they were eating grass while the battle was going on and our braves had no difficulty in catching all of them. While making our way to Poplar River these horses were not much good and we left a lot of them on the Missouri River."

Continuing, as he looked over the valley of the Little Big Horn from the high bluff where Custer's Final Stand was made, Gall said, "We knew where the soldiers camped on the night of June 24th. Buffalo scouts brought this word to us late at night on the 24th. We were surprised at this information, because we did not expect any soldiers unless they came from the South where we knew General Crook was. The buffalo scouts reported these soldiers to be northeast of us.

From I<small>NDIAN</small> N<small>OTES</small> <small>ON THE</small> C<small>USTER</small> B<small>ATTLE</small> *by*
David F. Barry.

Shot In The Eye—Oglala Sioux

"On the morning of the 25th away to the East, we saw soldiers marching down the divide in our direction. They passed out of sight behind the rough land several miles from the river. Just how these soldiers were divided, I do not know. We never saw the pack train (McDougall's Command) until it joined Reno on the hill.

"We first noticed several companies of soldiers about two miles east of our camp, marching along the bluffs in the direction of the lower end of our camp. These soldiers kicked up lots of dust and they came in sight the second time about two hours after noon. They were mounted on white horses and it was a nice sight to see this parade across the river to our East. We watched these soldiers and were rounding up our pony herd so we could fight if the soldiers attacked us. We did not know who was leading these men at that time. We were sure it wasn't Crook, because he didn't have so many white horses. As these soldiers marched along on the high land going Northwest and not directly toward us, we were not sure whether they meant to fight.

"Our camp was over two miles long and on the West bank of the Little Big Horn; in some places a long distance from the water. The valley was wide where we camped. The Black-feet Sioux (Not Montana Black-feet) were in the extreme South of the camp; the Hunkpapas, under Sitting Bull, White Bull, and One Bull were next; then came the Minneconjous; next the Oglalas; next the Brules and to the East of them and well toward the river were the San Arcs; and last were the Cheyennes at the extreme north end of camp.

"The soldiers we were watching were headed for the camp of the Cheyennes. While we were thus watching them, some boys who were out Southeast of the camp ran into the Black-feet camp and told them soldiers were coming from the Southeast and had shot at them. Very soon we heard a great amount of shooting in that direction. Crazy Horse rushed through our camp headed in the direction of the shooting and his men followed; I started that way to, and so did Crow King. We paid no attention to the soldiers marching toward the North end. About two thousand warriors finally gathered down where the shooting was (Reno's Command.)

"There was one force of Arikara scouts with this band of soldiers and they were on our right as we sped in that direction. We charged them first because it made us mad to see Indians fighting us. They ran first and we never saw them again. We turned toward our left to fight the soldiers. They were hard to drive out because they were on foot and in the brush and grass. We could not shoot them, so we charged them and soon they were trying to get on their horses. Those that were successful, ran almost straight east and crossed the river and got up on a high hill (Reno Hill). We killed many while they were fighting with their horses, and we killed many while they were running as our ponies were more speedy. We must have killed fifty men while they were running for the hill. (The actual number was 36.)

"As soon as we had chased these soldiers out, (Reno's Force), we did not fight them again right away. Crow King and Crazy Horse were afraid the soldiers that we had seen march in the direction of the north end of the camp, might kill our women and children. They went back the way they had come; their ponies were racing. Crow King turned to the right before he got to the North end and got in a deep gully and those soldiers (Custer's) could not see the warriors. Ride down there and you will see that this gulley is so deep that no one can see you from here. This gulley, the upper part, brought Crow King very close to the soldiers. Crazy Horse went to the extreme north end of the camp and then turned to his right and went up another very deep ravine and by following it, which he did, he came very close to the soldiers on their north side. Crow King was on their south side. This bunch of soldiers were headed directly for our camp and were about half way between the place where these graves are and the river. They, Custer, never crossed the river.

"It was about a little after 2:30 P.M. when this part of the battle began. Crow King shot from the South and Crazy Horse from the North. The soldiers were trying to get back up the hill, but Crazy Horse and his warriors were behind the top of the hill shooting. Soldiers were falling all around; they were on foot and their horses were in the upper end of the ravine where Crazy Horse was.

"I saw what was going on, and left the hill, Reno Hill, and ran for the battle. I struck the trail the soldiers had made as they marched down to the North end and soon came up to some of them to the east of where the rest were. (He means East of Custer.) We either killed or ran over these and went on down to where the last soldiers were. They were fighting good. The men were loading and firing, but they could not hit the warriors in the gulley and the ravine. The dust and smoke was black as evening. Once in a while we could see the soldiers through the dust, and finally we charged through them with our ponies. When we had done this, right here on this ground, just a few rods South of us, the fight was over. While all this fighting was going on, a part of the warriors were catching the soldiers' horses. Not all were fighting. We had all the horses before the battle was over except some few which we caught. We killed all the men who were holding the horses.

"There was one soldier on a hill southeast of us still firing when the battle ended, and we had a hard time to kill him. He killed several of our braves. Finally some of the braves crawled up the hill on all of the four sides. While he was killing some in front of him, those behind him finally killed him. (This evidently was Sergeant Butler.)

"As soon as the fight was over here, I went back toward those soldiers on the high hill, Reno's Command. We met some of them coming toward us, but we had too many men; they had to run back with the rest. I wanted to attack these soldiers, but the medicine men said we had killed enough. They said that the medicine wasn't right yet. The warriors believed this, but I always thought a good gun was the strongest kind of medicine. We didn't fight these soldiers much, but kept shooting away at them that afternoon and the next day. Every time they would crawl up in sight, we would shoot at them.

"Sitting Bull was trying to round up the ponies when the fight started against the soldiers (Reno's Command), but I did not see him anywhere I was fighting, but he said we had killed enough soldiers and to not kill those on the hill."

*   *   *   *

Barry, in his notes, says this about Gall; "Gall's face is admitted to be the strongest face among the American Indians." The following is what Mrs. Elizabeth Custer, the late General's wife, said about the picture of Gall in a letter she wrote me after I had sent her his photograph. 'Mr. Barry: As painful as it is for me to look upon the pictured face of an Indian, I never dreamed in all my life that there could be in all the tribes, so fine a specimen for a warrior as Chief Gall.' That is saying a great deal, coming from Mrs. Custer.

"Look well at the strong-powerful face of Chief Gall and you will not wonder why the Custer fight lasted only thirty-five minutes. We often hear it remarked that Custer took the Sioux by surprise. This is foolish talk. Could you catch Chiefs as Gall, Rain-in-the-Face, and Crazy Horse loafing when they knew the soldiers were in that country? On the 17th day of June under the leadership of Crazy Horse, they had given that famous Indian fighter, General Crook, quite a little skirmish. He loved his men too well to sacrifice them. He plainly saw that there were too many Indians. He wisely retreated rather than sacrifice his soldiers. The Custer fight took place on the 25th of June, a little over a week after they gave General Crook a little fight. Every now and then, some brilliant writer tells how Custer took the Indians by surprise. The little group of men who stood on Custer Battlefield, the evening of June 24, 1886 listened to Chief Gall relate that awful story of the fight, failed to hear him say that Custer and his men took them by surprise. There is one big mistake which is always made and that is that the Sioux were always underestimated as fighters. I say give them plenty of ammunition and good rifles that they are familiar with in regard to loading and with such chiefs as Gall to lead them, they do not know what fear is. They are good shots, good riders, and once in action, they fear nothing. Thus equipped, I would place them against an equal number of any cavalry in the world. I know of only one

83

cavalry force of equal numbers that might make them hit the back trail, and that cavalry they regard with respect—the cavalry of the United States.

"Chief Gall was a modest Indian—no blow or show to him. His word was as good as his bond. In the winter of 1880, Major Ilges held a council with him at Poplar, Montana, and asked him and his Indians to come in and surrender. Gall answered, 'I will fight rather than surrender.' Major gave him so many hours to think the matter over, and if he preferred to fight after that hour, he would accommodate him. Gall did not come in and the soldiers opened fire. The Indians returned the fire compliment with considerable force. The Major ordered Gatling guns cut loose. Every shot seemed to touch a tender spot in their hearts. The Indians made a slide close to the earth, and soon a white flag was seen waving through the brush in the timber. The Sioux regard the Gatling gun with considerable respect. They certainly did bow to it.

"When Gall returned to Standing Rock Agency, he took fate kindly. He commanded the respect of every one who knew him, both whites and Indians. I dare make the bold statement that his agent, Major James McLaughlin, will say he was the best Indian in the whole reservation. Had he lived to be a hundred years old, the Indians would have been better for his being."

"And yet, they wonder at the fate of Custer. Go over the battlefield, live with the Sioux long enough to know them, then pull yourself together; think, and you won't wonder.

"Gall was the justice of the Indian Police Court at Standing Rock Agency. There is no justice in any court of the United States that could give you the limit with more solemn dignity than Chief Gall. He is one of the type that should live for two hundred years."

Curley—scout for Gen. Custer   *Running Antelope—Dakota Sioux*

Sioux Ghost Dancers

Dark Eye—Sioux girl

Photos—Barry (opp.), courtesy Pettigrew Museum, (top and right) Nebraska State Hist. Soc.

Chief Gall as a Hostile

Barry's noted photograph of Chief Gall was made immediately after his capture in the winter of 1881 by a part of General Miles' Regiment, the Fifth Infantry, together with a part of the Seventh Cavalry, which had been Custer's Command. Gall, with other chiefs after a sharp brush fight which required the use of a Gattling gun to end in favor of the soldiers, surrendered and were brought to Fort Buford as prisoners of war. Shortly after their arrival, the "Little Shadow-Catcher," with the assistance of money and one officer, and Dan Allison, a scout, got Chief Gall to his gallery just as he had come in. Refusing to listen to suggestions to pose, he stood before the camera as best suited him. Later he returned to the gallery alone and asked to see the picture. Being shown the plate, which was all that was finished, he declared that it was "bad" and he wanted to destroy it. Feeling that something of the kind was in the wind, the photographer had put the plate back in the dark room and when he refused to get it, the chief started to find it himself.

Realizing that all his work was about to go for nothing, the "Little Shadow-Catcher" pushed the Indian to one side. Quick as a flash, the Indian, furious, drew a knife, and as quick the photographer covered him with his revolver, which laid on a shelf. Pausing for a few moments in indecision, apparently attempting to fathom the determination of the holder of the revolver, Gall backed slowly out of the gallery and the picture was safe. Gall died in 1893.

Gall became quite fat during his later years and tried out a fat-reducing remedy which some friend had recommended. He took this medicine methodically for about a week, but the promised reduction in weight did not materialize. Gall argued that if a little of this medicine would reduce him "some," the whole bottle would bring about the results he wanted. He, accordingly, drank the full contents of the bottle, the results of which proved fatal. Gall died on the 5th day of December, 1893, and was buried at Wakpala, South Dakota. There is a marble marker over his grave reading:

> John Gall, Chief of the Hunkpapa Sioux,
> Born on Grand River, Dakota, about
> 1840, and Died, December 5, 1893.

Photo—Barry, courtesy Pettigrew Museum

Chief Gall's camp, 1881

Chief Gall

Three views of famous Sioux warrior

These photographs of Chief Gall as he looked when a hostile, were all taken by David F. Barry after his capture in 1881. Gall led the Sioux as they swept down upon Custer's Command at the Little Big Horn in June 1876 and wiped it out of existence. How the pictures were made is explained in the text opposite.

Photos—Barry (two top), courtesy Nebraska State Hist. Soc., (right) Pettigrew Museum

Photographer David F. Barry,
known to the Sioux as "Little Shadow Catcher," posed with Rain In The Face.

Photo—Barry, courtesy Nebraska State Hist. Soc.

Rain In The Face

"On June 25, 1886," related David F. Barry, "I stood on the Custer Battlefield close to Gall and listened to the awful story of that battle as he related it. No soldier who was in the Custer Engagement ever lived to tell that story.

"In that little bunch stood General Godfrey, Captain McDougal, Captain Benteen, Dr. Porter, Colonel Partello, and Captain Edgerly. As Partello has often said, the visit to the field was one of the events of his life. The crowd was as silent as the dead that were sleeping on the field except the voice of Gall who was telling the awful story of the battle.

Most of those mentioned here have passed over that old trail that leads over the divide to the great beyond. The public has read of the Indian Generals who took part in that fight, Gall, Sitting Bull, Crow King, and Crazy Horse, and others. I shall here aim to tell the prominent part that Rain-in-the-Face took prior to the Custer Battle and during it to the finish.

"The foundation and cornerstone to the cause of the Custer Fight that took place on June 25, 1876, can best be told by giving the story of Rain-in-the-Face and his activities prior to the Custer Battle.

"Dr. Holzinger, who was the veterinary surgeon, and Mr. Balarian, who was the sutler with Custer, fell behind the Command to pick up specimens along the Yellowstone. Rain-in-the-Face, who had been watching the movements of the troops, noticed these two men fall behind the Command looking as if they were trying to find something. He watched the troops pass out of sight. Well armed as he was with a good Winchester and the troops out of sight, he could not over-look two good shots. Taking good aim, he shot one of the men. The other turned to see where the shot was fired from; quick as a flash, Rain-in-the-Face shot him dead.

"The killing of those two men was a mystery. Over a year after this killing, the Sioux were having a Big Dance at Standing Rock Agency. After each dance, some brave would walk into the circle and tell about his bravery. After one of these dances, a dashing, fine-looking young chief stepped into the circle and told them just how he had shot those two men on the Yellowstone. After he had finished his story, he received great applause from the thousands of Indians who had listened while he told them of his bravery. Charlie Reynolds, General Custer's scout, stood silent listening to Rain-in-the-Face relate the mysterious killing of those two men. "Lonesome" Charlie, as he was called, returned to Fort Lincoln and told General Custer that he had heard Rain-in-the-Face tell how he had killed Dr. Holzinger and Mr. Balarian.

"The next ration day, he sent Captain Tom Custer, his brother, with one hundred men of the 7th Cavalry to Standing Rock to arrest Rain-in-the-Face for the killing. Tom Custer looked around for some time to find Rain-in-the-Face. He located him in the old Trader's Store. Armed with a Winchester, he, Custer, slipped up behind him and grabbed both of his arms. With the help of some of the soldiers, they started with him for Fort Lincoln, and placed him in the Guard House to be tried by the United States Court.

"One night when they were blowing 'taps,' two men, who had been stealing grain from Fort Lincoln and waiting there to have their trial, broke out of the Guard House. When the second one was crawling out, he motioned to Rain-in-the-Face to come on. Rain-in-the-Face told me that the guard saw them going, but he did not order them to halt, but kept on walking back and forth with his rifle on his shoulder. Rain-in-the-Face said that

This sketch is from the booklet INDIAN NOTES ON THE CUSTER BATTLE *by David F. Barry, pioneer Indian photographer known to the Sioux as "Little Shadow Catcher," as edited by Usher L. Burdick.*

he expected he would shoot at him. He also says that the men were assisted in getting out, and they saw them walk away.

"When he got on the other side of the hill, he started on the run for Standing Rock. At the break of day, he crawled under some brush and remained there all day. It took him part of two nights to reach his people at Standing Rock. They got a war party together of young braves and started him out into the hills. As they were sure that Custer would come and look for him.

"Very few of them ever came into the Agency. They had grown so treacherous and bold that an expedition was sent out in the spring of 1876 to arrest and have all these Indians returned to the agencies. Chief Rain-in-the-Face was the leader of this little band of hostiles that had increased from a few to thousands. When he heard in May 1876 that Custer and his command had left Ft. Lincoln to capture and return him and the other hostile Indians to the Reservations, the news spread like wildfire, and the Indians kept coming from all the agencies until they were so strong and well armed that we did not fear the soldiers. They all got together on the Little Big Horn ready and waiting to fight. More Indians than he had seen together ever before at one time. 'They were wild for battle,' he said.

"They had watched Custer for days. Indians would come in and tell where they had camped, but they had got to the Little Big Horn sooner than they expected. Rain-in-the-Face kept thinking all the time, 'I will get you,' meaning Tom Custer. He said he was not a brave, he was a coward and afraid of him. He said that he always thought he would catch him some time. Tom Custer's body, when found on the battlefield, was so horribly mutilated that it was a mere accident that it was identified by Dr. Porter, General Godfrey, and General Benteen. He also said that he wished he had gone to the battlefield on the Tenth Anniversary and shown me and told me there so I could understand. He admired General Custer as a Big Chief. He always said that Mrs. Custer was a good woman. Strange, he would often ask about her, but for Tom Custer, hate is a mild word.

"The world knows the fate of General Custer and his five companies of the 7th Cavalry on that expedition. It is not my intention to show Rain-in-the-Face as a brave hero, but with all his savage nature, he possessed a good heart and valued a true friend.

"This cruel savage, as he was called, when I left the West, took his moccasins off his feet and gave them to me, requesting me to keep them as long as I lived, and when I looked at them to think of him. When he shook hands and said goodbye, he said: 'My heart is on the ground.'

"On September 12, 1905, just ten minutes before he died, he said he wanted to say goodbye to me and shake my hand. He would pray and do what he could for me on the other side. This is the savage, Rain-in-the-Face, we hear of now days in song and story, who was the truest friend I ever had and with all his savage nature, he possessed a good heart and valued a true friend. His life was anything but pleasant. He accidentally shot himself while hunting Buffalo, North of Woody Mountain, Canada, crippling him for life, the loss of his son, and his second squaw who would drive the cold steele into him in a jealous rage.

"We are often asked, 'Did you ever know of a Sioux Indian that you could have the faith and confidence in that you would have in your white friend?' One of the most savage and treacherous of the Sioux Indians was the truest friend I ever had, either white or red man. This may be a broad statement, but I am willing to confess and admit that I would trust him sooner than any other white friend I ever had. It is remarkable when you know he was savage and cruel; he seemed to worship a good, true friend. While he was a prisoner in the Guard House at Fort Lincoln, Mrs. Elizabeth Custer, the late General's wife, took an interest in him and was good and kind to him. He never forgot that kindness. In late years he would inquire after her; ask if she were still living, and if she remarried, saying she was a good woman. He would like to take her hand, admitting he shot Dr. Holzinger and Balarian off their horses in a most cowardly manner. Again the whites are just as cowardly when at war.

"President Cleveland appointed three Commissioners composed of Captain Pratt, Judge Weight of Washington and Reverend Cleveland, to get the Sioux to sign a treaty that had been drawn up by Congress. The Commissioners held their councils in a warehouse, 300 by 80 feet. It was impossible to get a photo of that Council in the building. I said to Rain-in-the-Face, 'Captain Pratt treats you Indians like a lot of school children, when you know all the great Councils and treaties were held outside under the sun with the sky for a covering. You are packed in that building like cattle; the air is bad. Insist tomorrow that the Council meeting be held outside like your fore-fathers. Mention this tonight at the Council at your camp, but don't mention my name.'

"The Commissioners met the next morning at 10:00 A.M. Not a single Indian in the building; Captain Pratt sent the interpreter over to tell them to come in and that the Commissioners were ready to talk. Mad Bear sent back word if he wanted to talk to them he would have to hold his Council outside under the sky, where all their great Councils had been held to do business. They were forced to move out under the sun. Captain Pratt doesn't know to this day that Rain-in-the-Face was the leader of that move. The Council was photographed in 1890.

"The last place in the world the average person would look for an exemplification of unchanging, true-to-the-end friendship, would be within the heart of one from a people who have come to be known as synonymous to all that is crafty and cruel. The American Indian has always been looked upon as the embodiment of all that is bad, the feeling having been expressed in the jest quoted: 'The only good Indian is a dead Indian,' and to the Sioux has been given the credit of proving its truth. All the more wonder, then, that one of this proud race should put his white brothers to shame in a friendship which stopped only at the brink of the grave, and even then promised not to lapse into forgetfulness on 'the other side.'

"Has the Sioux any loyalty and affection for his white friends?"

A South Dakota newspaper makes the following comment on the death of Rain-in-the-Face, in 1905:

"News comes from Grand River, North Dakota, of the death there, Monday, of that celebrated Sioux warrior, Rain-in-the-Face, who was one of the leaders in the Custer massacre. He was 63 years of age, and had been an Indian policeman for many years. The famous Sioux and David F. Barry, of Superior, were great friends, the latter having helped to get the Indian his police appointment at Standing Rock. Mr. Barry had known Rain-in-the-Face since 1875 or 1876, and the grim red man liked much the frontier photographer in the early days. Among the many famous men, both red and white, that Mr. Barry came to know there, he has always admired Rain-in-the-Face. The Indian called the Superior man, in the Sioux tongue, the 'Little Shadow Catcher.'

"I was sorry to hear of the death of Rain-in-the-Face," said Mr. Barry last evening. "He was a great Indian, and he has been grossly maligned in some respects. It has been so widely published that it is hardly possible to contradict it now, that Rain-in-the-Face killed Custer and then cut his heart out. I investigated that story, and did it early, and found that it was not true. Rain-in-the-Face has often talked with me about that report. It has worried him that the public should accept it as true. Now that he is dead, we may look for a recurrence of the libel on the old chief. He was a great warrior and a typical Sioux. He has killed many white men, no doubt, but that story of his cutting Captain Tom Custer's heart out, should not be allowed to go undisputed. There are several men living who are ready to prove what I say.

"Mr. Barry is full of reminiscenses touching on the dead redman, and the days during which his friendship with him was begun."

The following comment was taken from the Duluth *News Tribune*, February 20, 1934:

"The death of Gall, the famous Sioux Chief, leaves John Grass the most commanding figure in the Sioux nation. Grass was for years chief justice at the Standing Rock Indian Agency and during the negotiations for the opening of 11,000,000 acres of the reservation to settlement, was the Indian spokesman. During the memorable debate between the Government Commissioners and Grass, the eloquent and diplomatic Indian so completely proved his intellectual superiority over Chairman Pratt of that Commission that there remained no room to doubt his ability and tact. He is a fine specimen of the Sioux and his leadership is such as the Indians may safely follow and the Government unhesitatingly indorse."

Chief Old Wolf

*Good Horse—
reservation
policeman*

Photos—Barry (left), courtesy U. of
Wyoming, (below) Pettigrew Museum,
(opp.) Nebraska State Hist. Soc.

Chief Long Dog

Chief Goos

Sitting Bull

"This stalwart Sioux character," wrote Warren K. Moorehouse, an early day magazine correspondent, "was killed Dec. 12, 1891, while resisting arrest at the Standing Rock Reservation where he lived. He was brave in the sense that a wild beast is brave when cornered and knows no alternative but to fight; so when Indian police came to arrest him he drew two Colt's revolvers and shot two or three men before they killed him.

"Sitting Bull was a prominent doctor, making medicine for the Custer fight and it was his bands who were instrumental in keeping the whites out of the Black Hills for so many years. Some eastern papers picture him as a mighty warrior, leading hosts to battle, performing prodigies of valor and inciting followers to deeds of daring heroism. He was not a warrior at all but a shaman, priest or medicine man. His mission was to make medicine for the Sioux before beginning a fight. When successful the crafty old chief was quick to let it be known about the village that this was due to the virtues of the medicine he had furnished. His following was in the northern tribes only. In the Pine Ridge area there was no respect for him. Even in his own village his people never accorded to him the importance he attached to himself and to which he felt fairly entitled. He loved to pose as a great man, one to whose counsel and bravery the tribe owed success in battle or raids. He was always to be found in the lead of a charge and his voice was the loudest in urging any measure until a danger line was reached and then he prudently took to safe retreat.

"After a battle or foray in which adversaries were worsted, he would walk over the scene and among the fallen enemy with looks of scorn on his face and a haughty air as though all this was due to his own good work. But if he was only a pretender as a warrior, he undoubtedly possessed great skill in laying plans for others to carry out; as a wily strategist he was very successful and to this fact we may ascribe his ascendancy among his people which, far from as great as the newspaper stories would have it, was still one of high degree."

Photos—Barry (left), courtesy Nebraska State Hist. Soc., (right) Pettigrew Museum

Rain In The Face—famous Sioux warrior   *Chief Red Horse*

Sitting Bull

who made medicine for Custer fight.
Below (left to right), John Sitting Bull,
Standing Holy, Crow Foot — Sitting
Bull's sons and daughter.

Photos—Barry, all courtesy Pettigrew
Museum except (lower right) Nebraska
State Hist. Soc.

Chief Wild Horse, cousin of Crazy Horse

96

Chief Low Dog

Photos—Barry (right), courtesy U. of Wyoming, (below) Pettigrew Museum

Thunder Hawk

American Horse

Chapter Nine

DULL KNIFE'S 1878 CHEYENNE RAID

I T WAS in September, 1878, that I had come into the then flourishing town of Ellsworth, Kansas. It was then the terminus of the Texas Trail herds that would be shipped from there to Kansas City. Other thousands passed on to the northern ranges by different routes. Ellsworth was then a wild sort of place infested by some of the worst characters on the western frontier. Most of the Texas Trail hands that had hired for this place wanted to go back after the cattle had been disposed of. But at this time there was a Mr. Blackman who had bought two thousand steers that had to be delivered to Kearney, Nebraska, so he found it hard to pick up a trail crew of the right kind of men. I hired to him as a horse wrangler. He had eight other men and a negro cook, a long lank black fellow, but some cook, always had his mouth open and always singing. Tom had a pair of mules and a covered wagon, but no tent.

We started off to the northwest so as to get west of the settlements, but Blackman thought we could cross the heads of the Prairie Dog, Sappa, and Beaver Creeks and not go so far west. So we swung into the head of the Prairie Dog Creek and were going down a long divide towards the creek. Tom was ahead with the mess wagon and I was close to him with the horse gang, when Tom stopped and I rode up to him. He had stopped his singing for the time. We looked down on one of as nice a scene as I ever saw. The stream was skirted with timber, with a fine string of farms along the stream. That part of it was sure fine, but there was more to it. Something seemed out of place. There were bands of horses scattered here and there with camps along the creek, with the camp fires sending up long columns of smoke. That was what had first drawn our attention to the scene. Then Blackman rode up to us and asked why we did not camp, when Tom pointed to the valley

A stirring episode of Indian frontier history concerns the famous Cheyenne raid of 1878 under Chief Dull Knife. After their first great defeat by Colonel MacKenzie in November, 1876, many of the Northern Cheyennes came to Ft. Robinson and surrendered, being then sent south under military escort to Oklahoma Territory. Having lived on the high plains at the foot of the Rocky Mountains in natural freedom, they were oppressed, mentally and physically, in the southern confinement, many dying from sickness.

In September, 1878, some three hundred men, women and children broke away from the armed guards and led by Chief Dull Knife, started north to the old hunting grounds. They created a reign of terror in Western Kansas and Nebraska, killing settlers and destroying property. They reached Ft. Robinson and gave themselves up but were kept under guard, again breaking away on January 9, 1879. Troops pursued the bands and desperate fighting occurred in the badlands and broken region near the head of White River. Out of the hundred and fifty escaping from the fort, sixty-four were killed, fifty-eight sent to the Cheyenne Agency, twenty returned to Oklahoma and a few dying in the hills.

The personal account given here is that of settler A. N. Keith and appeared in NEBRASKA HISTORY, *Vol. 7, No. 4.*

Brule war party

Photo—Curtis, courtesy Seattle Public Library

and camp. Blackman was an old Texan and his jaws snapped like a steel trap when he said, "Injins, them runaway Cheyennes and they are on the warpath, too."

Another minute we had seen a string of Indians start in our direction. They were going up the draws on both sides of us. That was enough and Blackman said to Tom, "Unhitch the team," but Tom was pulling the harness off the mules, and was just mounting the dun mule when Blackman said, "Tom, that mule ain't broke to ride." Tom said, "Mister, maybe he ain't but he sure will be mighty quick," and then I noticed Tom had turned almost white and his eye bulged out and he could hardly talk. He was the whitest nigger that I have ever seen, but he sure stayed with that mule. We three rode back till we met the herd. The Indians were crowding us hoping to cut us off and get the horse cavvy. But when we joined the other eight men they drew off to one side. When four men rode out toward them they fired at them and tried to ride between them and the rest of us and then the other bunch came up from the other side and stampeded the herd and a small bunch had captured the wagon. Our outfit only carried six guns in all, forty-four or forty-five revolvers, so were not a very warlike outfit and had the Indians known that they might have had more scalps the next day.

By this time it was near sundown and we could hear the crack of rifles down toward the camp and we knew that the Indians would have plenty of beef for supper. When we got back we found about eighty steers that they had killed that night, so the only thing for us to do was to ride south to the railroad some thirty miles. When we rode into Buffalo station towards morning we found the town in a state of excitement I had never seen before. The Cheyennes had broken away from the reservation and on their way north, but no one knew where they were until we came in and told what had happened to us. When we had run into them they had done no killing up to that time, but the next morning the massacre began in earnest. Our little brush with them and the killing of the beef cattle gave the settlers close there a chance to escape. They burned everything that would burn on the Prairie Dog, Sappa, and Beaver Creeks. I do not remember how many men were killed, but I remember the case of young Abbot. He had gone out after his horse when the Indians caught up to him and shot him. His father heard the shots and taking his gun went out to see what was up when the Indians showed up in the timber along the creek. They called to him to stop and talk but he ran towards the dugout with bullets biting all around him. He entered the dugout and dug a hole through a window that had been filled up with sod and opened fire on the bunch. He killed two horses and one Indian had his hip broken so he was left to die or maybe he was left for dead. But he hid and was not found for sometime. Later on some men were looking over the scene and found that some one was cutting the flesh of the dead horses and then they began to search the timber and found an Indian with his hip broken. So someone shot him and scalped him. He had a long braid of coal black hair as thick as one's wrist and three feet long. I do not know what became of it, but just a few years ago an old friend in Beaver City asked me what I had done with that Indian scalp that I got on the Beaver.

Another case I remember was the two girls, sisters. I will not mention their names for they are both living yet. They were captured and outraged in the most brutal manner and kept with the Indians for two or three days, then stripped naked and turned loose. They were found by a cowboy and taken to the nearest settlement.

There had been a large band of cowboys formed to follow the Indians. They were held up by the soldiers and soldiers are not much good to chase Indians if they try to do it with wagons. If the cowboys had gone the Indians would never have gotten to the Platte river. Just before they reached the Platte river they split up in small bands and all dispersed. There was one bunch of eight or nine that was waylaid by a bunch of cowboys and were all killed. On the divide north of the Beaver we found an old man who had been left behind. He was old and almost blind and toothless, must have been a hundred years old. They had been carrying him in travois and it had broken down and he had been left to die. The boys were discussing what to do with him when some one said to remember young Abbott and then some one grabbed the end of the travois pole and the old warrior drew the blanket over his face and the cowboy hit him with the club and killed him. This was close to the place where a few years before a lieutenant and four men were killed by the Indians. They had been surrounded by Indians and had killed their horses for breastworks and had all been killed, mutilated, stripped naked and then pinned to the ground with arrows. That was all the Indians that we overtook on the trip. They made their way up north and were captured somewhere in Wyoming or Dakota. The winter they were being held prisoners at Ft. Robinson, Nebraska was a very cold winter and all the warriors broke out and got away but were rounded up in the badlands and they fought until the last one died. They were the Northern Cheyennes, known as Dull Knife's band. Dull Knife was killed in the winter of 1876-77 on the Red fork of Powder River and his whole camp equipage was burned that time. They were captured and taken to Oklahoma. Then they raided Kansas on their way back to Wyoming. After all the warriors were killed at Ft. Robinson the women and children were taken back to Oklahoma. But after a few years they all drifted back to the north and located on the Rosebud in Montana, where they have stayed about as peaceable as a Cheyenne could. They agreed to behave themselves if the Government would let them stay. They were the finest and most virtuous Indians as well as the fiercest in war. If you see any half-breed Cheyennes you will know they bear a white man's name and that honestly. There are no illegitimate children among the Northern Cheyennes.

The Cheyennes were kept in the guard house at Fort Robinson, Nebraska, that winter of 1878. The warriors all broke out and got into the bad lands, but were overtaken by the soldiers and they fought until the last one was killed. One of the soldiers who is still living in Rawlins, Wyo., told me of the fight. He said that when they were captured and gave up their guns they concealed the best of them by taking them apart and the squaws hid them under their clothes. He told me that the first time they struck the Indians was where the Chicago & Northwestern Rail Road crosses the creek at the edge of the Fort and they left fourteen dead Indians on the bank of the creek. He told me that every time that the soldiers had a brush with them that there were one or two soldiers shot square in the mouth. There was one Indian that was a sure dead shot. There was a gambler in Buffalo station heard me tell Blackman that I wanted to follow the cowboys after the Cheyennes, but I had no horse when he said "come here" and he gave me an order for his horse with the remark, "he is a good one and if I never see you or Old Soll again, good-bye." I kept Soll for a long time but I never saw the old gambler again.

Prairie cabin in Dakota Territory

Chief He Dog

*He Dog's daughter at Pine
Ridge Reservation*

Photos courtesy Nebraska State Hist. Soc.

Young Calf

Painting Horse

Chief Black Horn

Chief Stinking Bear

Sioux Sun Dancer

As they danced, the performers never left the spot on which they stood, springing slightly upward from the toes and ball of feet, legs and body rigid. The right palm was always extended to the glaring sun, eyes fixed upon the lower rim of it. The dancer concentrated his mind, his very self, upon the one thing he desired whether it was acquiring a powerful medicine or success in the next conflict.

Photos (opp.)—Curtis, courtesy Seattle Public Library, (above left) Nebraska State Hist. Soc., (right) Wyoming State Archives

*Hector Crawler—
Stoney chief*

*Cheyenne Chief
Feathered Wolf*

Black Coal

Chief Two Elk

Chapter Ten

ATTACK on FORT LARAMIE

THE OVERLAND stage company had quite an important station at Julesburg, on the south side of the river, about a mile east of the location of Fort Sedgwick. It was in 1865 before any rails had been laid on the Union Pacific. The stage company had accumulated a large quantity of supplies at this station, and the Indians knowing this and ever hostile to the travel of whites through this region, had their cupidity aroused. Troops were scattered all along the route and frequently had to escort the stages from one station to another. At Julesburg the road crossed the South Platte, followed the Lodge Pole up to Sidney, and then crossed over the North Platte which ascended to Fort Laramie and beyond.

Capt. N. J. O'Brien was in command of the fort with one company of the Seventh Iowa Cavalry and two pieces of artillery. On the 7th of January, The Sioux and Cheyennes, one thousand strong, discovering the small force defending it, attacked the fort with great bravery. They had previously run the stage into the station killing one man.

When their presence was discovered, Capt. O'Brien made the best disposition possible with his small force. He left a sergeant with twelve men in the fort to handle the artillery, and mounting the rest, twenty-seven men and one officer beside himself, went out to meet the savages. The charge was sounded and in they went. About a mile from the fort there is a projecting hill in the bluffs, back of and around which the main body of the Indians was concealed. As the men neared the top of this hill they saw the large force opposed to them but they never flinched. The Indians charged upon them in great fury and for quite a time the unequal contest was continued. And when the captain ordered the men to fall back, they did so in good order, forced to leave their dead comrades to fall into the hands of the bloodthirsty foe. The Indians now attacked with greater fury, attempting to cut off the retreat. They did surround the soldiers but the artillery came into play, kept them at bay and night put an end to the battle.

In the morning there was not an Indian in sight. But now comes the most horrible part of this incident. The men went out to find, if possible, the bodies of their dead comrades. They found them but nearly all were beyond recognition; stripped of every vestige of clothing, mutilated beyond account, cold and stark they lay in the places they had fallen; their fingers, toes and ears cut off, their mouths filled with gunpowder and ignited, and every conceivable indignity commited upon their persons. Sorrowfully they gathered up these remains and conveyed them to the fort where they were decently buried; but the recollections of that awful night did not fade from the memories of the survivors. In subsequent battles with the savages, their courage was quickened and their arms nerved to deeds of daring, which cost many a warrior his life and gave him a sudden exit to his happy hunting grounds. The loss of the savages in this battle, could not, at the time, be

This account with others by Henry T. Williams,
appears in his PACIFIC TOURIST *of 1879.*

accurately ascertained but later the Indians admitted they had lost sixty-three warriors. None were found on the field as they always carry their dead away with them.

On the 2nd of February, less than a month from the above attack, they appeared in the vicinity of the fort again, attacked and burned the station house of the stage company, other outbuildings and stores, and one or two houses adjoining. Five miles below the station was a ravine called the Devil's Dive through which the stages passed. Capt. O'Brien and four or five men were escorting the coach with three or four passengers, one of whom was a lady. As he ascended the bank of the ravine going toward the fort, he saw a smoke, and riding to the top of a hill, he saw the Indians. Returning to the coach, he had every man, passengers and all, examine his arms and caused the coach to proceed slowly. Soon the road neared the bank of the river and here he met some teamsters with wagons, who beyond a pistol or two, were unarmed and greatly alarmed.

These men the captain ordered to return and keep near the stage, which they did, all moving slowly toward the station and fort. Meanwhile the heads of Indians were popping up quite frequently over the bluffs in the distance. Arriving near one of these the captain rode boldly to the top and taking his blanket, swung it three times over his head. The Indians saw this and supposed he had a large force in the rear which he was signalling to come up, and they began to fly. The river was frozen and sand had been scattered over two roadways on the ice. They took everything they could from the burning station and houses, and beat a retreat across the river. At the first sign of their leaving, the stage driver and teamsters put their animals to their utmost speed and ran into the fort, the captain arriving there in time to give the Indians a few parting shots from his artillery as the last of them ran across the river. The shots ricocheted along the ice and caused the Indians to drop some of their plunder, though doing no further damage, as we could learn.

Swift Bear—Brule Sioux

Sword—Oglala Sioux

110

Chief Charge On The
Hawk—Oglala Sioux

Black Foot—Sioux

Oglala Chief Red Shirt
and daughter Annie Red Shirt

Photos—Heyn & Matzen, courtesy
Smithsonian Inst.

Agent McGillicuddy Rebuffed

When Oglala Sioux Chief Red Cloud refused government education for the children of his people, Red Shirt (photo opposite page) was one of the subchiefs who took an active stand with him. This was in 1880 when Agent McGillicuddy started a school on the Pine Ridge reservation. Added to this effort to socialize the Sioux was the arrival of General James R. O'Bierne for the purpose of distributing farm lands to them.

Red Cloud opposed all such action and sat stubbornly in his camp across Big White Clay Creek from the Pine Ridge Agency. In nearby camps were the two Loafer bands headed by Chiefs Red Shirt and High Bear. To break Red Cloud's animosity and force him to cooperate, Agent McGillicuddy used the lever of free government goods—blankets, clothing, bolts of cloth, kettles, axes, knives and other camp equipment. These were placed in seven piles, one for each band of Oglala Sioux, and Red Cloud moved to parcel out the goods. McGillicuddy attempted to change this custom by making the distribution himself but met with such violent disapproval, he was forced to give way to Red Cloud's power and watch him hand out the annuities.

As a further rebuff to the agent, who tried to depose Red Cloud as chief and declare him no more important than the most common Indian on the reservation, an order came from Washington instructing him to build for this head chief of the Oglala Sioux a two-story house. When completed the house was far more imposing than McGillicuddy's modest single-story dwelling and the Sioux were convinced the Great Father believed Red Cloud a much bigger man than the boy acting as agent.

Brule Sioux Tricked by Flagrant Land Grab

After a long period of persuasion and cajolery, in 1889, the government men of the Sioux Commission were disheartened. They had failed to force the three head chiefs of Pine Ridge Agency to sign an agreement to sell their lands. With Red Cloud, Young Man Afraid Of His Horses and Little Wound standing firm against the proposal, there were only 158 signatures out of the 1,366 adult males at Pine Ridge. Wearily, the Sioux Commission moved to the small agencies on the Missouri River—Lower Brule and Crow Creek.

The leader of the Sioux at Lower Brule was Iron Nation (photo opposite page). Under heavy pressure from the land-hungry Dakota whites, his people were demoralized. In their distrust of the government, they feared all their lands would be taken yet they had some confidence in General Crook and were willing to listen to him. Iron Nation informed him of their fears and Crook attempted to persuade him they were unfounded. When this failed, Crook made a written promise that should the whites seize the Indian lands, the Sioux would be resettled on good lands in the Rosebud Reservation.

Iron Nation then permitted his name to be signed to the agreement and the other Indians eagerly followed his example. Pressed for time, the Sioux Commission departed for Crow Creek. It then appeared the promises made to Iron Nation and his followers amounted to little short of bribery.

General Crook was an upright and conscientious man, sensitive in matters of honor such as this and the Sioux had faith in his integrity. Yet he had committed himself to chicanery, had made one pledge after another to the Indians, which in considered judgment he must have known the officials in Washington would never carry out, would not vote the funds necessary for such plans.

The immediate results proved his pledge to Iron Nation as empty and faithless. All the Lower Brule lands were at once taken by the whites and when the effort was made to settle the Brule Sioux on the Rosebud, the Brules of that agency refused to yield any land to their cousins. Thus defrauded of their property the displaced Lower Brules in utter frustration could only live with the thought of General Crook's treachery.

Chief Iron Nation—Brule Sioux

Beaded headband

Photos (below) courtesy U. of Wyoming, (opp.) Shindler, Smithsonian Inst.

Mormon prairie family

Cheyenne squaw and papoose

Photos (top) courtesy Union Pacific R.R.,
(left) Nebraska State Hist. Soc.

Chapter Eleven

BATTLE with INDIANS at PLUM CREEK

In July, 1867, a train was ditched about four miles west of the Plum Creek Station by a band of southern Cheyennes under a chief called Turkey Leg. At a small bridge over a dry ravine they had lifted the rails from the ties—raising only one end of each rail—about three feet, piling up ties under them for support and firmly lashing the rails to them with wire cut from the telegraph lines. They were pretty cunning in this, thinking the iron would penetrate the cylinders on each side of the engine, yet disregarding the slight curve in the road at this point, they missed their calculations, as one of the rails did no execution whatever and the other went straight into and through the boiler.

After they had fixed the rails thus they retired to where the bench or second bottom slopes down to the first and there concealed themselves in the tall grass, waiting for the train. Before it left Plum Creek, a hand-car with three section men was sent ahead as a pilot. This car encountered the obstacle and ran into the ravine, bruising and stunning the men and frightening them so they were unable to signal the approaching train. The Indians rushed up and two of the men the least hurt ran away in the darkness of the night—it was a little past midnight—and hid in the grass. The other, more stunned by the fall of the car, was scalped by the savages, yet deliriously snatched the scalp from the Indian and fled into the darkness. He is now an employe of the railroad in Omaha.

But the fated train came on without any knowledge of what had transpired in front. As the engine approached the ravine, the headlight gleaming out in the darkness, the engineer, Brooks Bowers by name, but familiarly called "Bully Brooks" by the railroad men, saw that the rails were displaced, whistled "down brakes" and reversed his engine, but all too late to stop the train. The door of the fire-box was open, and fireman Hendershot was in the act of adding fuel to the flames when the crash came. He was thrown against the fire-box and literally roasted alive, nothing but a few of his bones being afterwards found. The engineer was thrown over the lever he was holding through the cab window some twenty feet, the lever ripping open his abdomen and when found he was sitting on the ground holding his bowels in with his hands.

Next to the engine were two flat cars loaded with brick and these were landed brick and all some thirty feet in front of the engine, while the box cars, loaded with freight were thrown upon the engine and around the wreck in great disorder. After a time these took fire and added horror to the scene. The savages now swarmed around the train and whooped and yelled in great glee. When the shock first came however, the conductor ran ahead on the north side of the track to the engine and there saw Bowers and Hendershot. He told them he must leave them and flag the second section of the train or it too would

Partial account of battle from the PACIFIC TOURIST *by Henry T. Williams, published in 1879. Plum Creek, Nebraska Territory, was a stage station on the overland trail, 231 miles west of Omaha. By the nature of the bluffs in the area, the Indians could wait out of sight for emigrant trains, attack swiftly and vanish behind the protecting cover.*

be wrecked. He did so and returned with it to Plum Creek. Arriving there in the middle of the night in vain did he try to get a force of men to proceed to the scene of the disaster. It was not until morning that they rallied, armed themselves and went out to the wreck, near ten o'clock.

The burning cars had fallen around the brave engineer, and while the fiery brands undoubtedly added to his agony, they had also ended his earthly existence. His blackened and charred remains only told of his suffering. The rescuing party found the train still burning—the Indians had obtained all the plunder they could carry and left in the early morning. From the cars not burned they rolled out boxes and bales of bright-colored flannels and calicos. Bolts of these goods they would loosen, and with one end tied to their ponies' tails, they would mount and start at full gallop up and down the prairie just to see the bright colors streaming in the wind behind them.

But the end of this affair was not yet. The avenging hand of justice was on the track of these blood-thirsty villains. In the spring of that year, by order of General Augur, then in command of the military department of the Platte, Major Frank North of Columbus, Nebraska, who had no little experience in the business was authorized to raise a battalion of two hundred Pawnee Indians, who were peaceable and friendly toward the whites, and whose reservation is near Columbus, for scouting duty. It was the old experiment of fighting the devil with fire to be tried over again. These scouts were to fight the various hostile bands of Sioux, Arapahoes and Cheyennes and assist in guarding the railroad and railroad builders. At the time this train was attacked, these scouts were scattered in small detachments along the line of the road between Sidney and Laramie Plains. General Augur was immediately notified of it and he telegraphed Major North to take the nearest company of his scouts to the scene of the disaster. At that time Major North was about fourteen miles west of Sidney, at the end of the track, and his nearest company was some twelve miles farther on. Mounting his horse he rode to their camp in about fifty minutes, got his men together, and leaving orders for the wagons to follow, returned and arrived at the end of the track at about four o'clock in the afternoon. By the time these men and horses were loaded on the cars the wagons had arrived and by five o'clock the train pulled out. At Julesburg they were attached to a passenger train and by midnight, or twenty-four hours after the disaster, he arrived at the scene. Meanwhile other white troops, stationed nearby, had arrived and at daybreak Major North took the trail to ascertain if the Indians involved were northern or southern Cheyennes. The sharp-sighted Pawnees soon struck a trail and found where the hostile band had crossed the river and abandoned some of their plunder. Since the trail led south to the Republican Valley, the Pawnees decided these hostiles must be southern Cheyennes.

Major North returned from this thirty-five mile scout and reported to General Augur at Omaha, receiving orders to remain on scout in the vicinity and wait for another raid. The wait was not long. In about ten days, one of the scouts came riding in to the Plum Creek camp from the bluffs to the south, reporting he had seen Indians making their way toward the old overland stage station. Now under observation, the Indians turned their horses loose in an old sod corral to feed and began preparations to remain all night.

But Major North wanted to find out just who they were before dark. At first determined to lead the reconnoiter party, he gave way to the insistent urging of Capt. James Murie to let him lead the party. Two other white officers were in the command — Lieut. Isaac Davis and a sergeant—of forty-eight Pawnees. The company marched south, crossed the Platte River, turned left and followed down the bank to within about a mile and a half of the creek. Here they were discovered by the camped southern Cheyennes.

They began no mount in hot haste, eager to fight what they thought were white soldiers and they were confident of victory—a hundred and fifty warriors against a small band of fifty-two. Forming an irregular line, they rushed to the conflict. Captain Murie's command, as soon as they found they were discovered, left the bushes on the river bank, went up into the road. As soon as the order to charge was given, the Pawnees set up their war whoop, slapped their breast with their hands and shouted "Pawnees!"

The opposing lines met on the banks of the creek through which the scouts charged with all their speed. The Cheyennes immediately broke and fled in great confusion, every man for himself. Then followed the chase, the killing and scalping, the Cheyennes taking their old trail to the Republican Valley in desperation to escape the deadly fire of the Pawnees. By nightfall, fifteen Cheyenne scalps had been taken as well as two prisoners, a squaw and a sixteen-year-old boy, the nephew of Chief Turkey Leg. Thirty-five horses and mules were also taken while not a man of the scouts command was hurt.

They arrived back at Plum Crek at midnight in a rain storm and were greeted with shouts and the Pawnees spent the rest of the night in scalp dances and wild revelry. The boy and squaw were kept in their camp until late in the season when a big council was held with the Brule Sioux, Spotted Tail's band, at North Platte, to make a new treaty. Hearing of this council, Chief Turkey Leg sent in a runner and offered to deliver up six white captives for the squaw and boy—understood to succeed Turkey Leg as chief.

After the exchange had taken place, the old chief would scarcely allow the boy to leave his sight—such was his attachment to him—and manifested his delight over his recovery in every possible way. The white captives released were two white sisters by the name of Thompson who lived near Grand Island, their twin brothers, a Norwegian girl taken on the Little Blue River and a white child born to one of these women during captivity.

The Indians however were not willing to have the iron rails that should bind the shores of the continent together laid in peace and made strenuous and persistent efforts to prevent it. On the 16th of April, 1868, a "cut off" band of Sioux, under a scalawag chief, Two Strikes, attacked and killed five section men near Elm Creek station, taking their scalps and a few head of stock. They were not pursued. On the same day, and apparently by prearranged plan, a part of the same band attacked the post at Sidney by coming up the bluffs on the north side of town and firing into it.

Two conductors, Tom Cahoon and William Edmundson, were fishing on Lodge Pole Creek, and were unobserved by the attacking Indians. Hearing the reports, they climbed up the banks to see what was going on, were seen by the Sioux who charged down upon them, shooting Cahoon. He fell forward on the ground, was scalped and left for dead. Edmunson ran for the post, firing at the savages with a small Derringer and escaped with arrow and bullet wounds, four arrows sticking in his body. His life was saved. After the Indians had gone, the citizens went after the body of Cahoon and to their amazement, found him still alive. They brought him into the post where he recovered and later went back to work on the railroad.

In September of the same year the same band of Sioux attempted to destroy a train between and Alkali and Ogalalla. They fixed the rails the same as at Plum Creek and the engine went into the ditch in similar fashion, the cars piling up on top of it.

The engineer and a brakeman who was in the engine at the time were thrown through the window of the cab but little hurt. The fireman was burned to death. All the trains at this time carried arms and the conductor, with two or three passengers, among them Father Ryan, a Catholic priest of Columbus, seized the arms and defended the train from the Indians skulking among the bluffs and firing occasionally.

Major North was then at Willow Island and was ordered to follow the Indians with one company of his scouts. He came to Alkali and reported to Colonel Mizner, who was marching from North Platte with two companies of cavalry, all of whom started in pursuit. They went over to the North Platte River, crossed it and entered the sand hills where they overtook the Indians and killed two of them. Thirty-five miles on they found where the main body had camped, smouldering embers of their fires still alive. During the night some of the white soldiers let their fires get away and started an immense prairie fire. This, of course, alarmed the Indians and further pursuit was abandoned.

119

Sioux near Ft. Laramie, 1868.
Left to right: Lone Horn, Pipe, Grass, Young Elk.

Chief Grass—
Pride of Standing Rock

The Standing Rock Indian Agency had no stauncher friend and worker for peace with the Indians than Chief Grass (in group above) and the heads of other agencies looked in vain for others like him. In twenty years the wild Sioux warrior and hunter had transformed himself into a hard working Christian farmer, standing loyal to the government.

The Standing Rock Sioux were united in opposition to the sale of their lands, proposed in 1883 by the land commission. They were attempting to farm and had a deeper feeling against the sale than did the more freedom loving Sioux of the Rosebud and Pine Ridge reservations. They also felt more keenly the government's failure to carry out some of the terms of earlier agreements.

Standing Rock agent James McLaughlin approved of the land sale and being well liked and trusted by the Sioux in his jurisdiction they were confused and perturbed when he began to coax and persuade them to sign the agreement. The land commission blindly refused to recognize any opposition and used all possible forms of pressure to break down what it encountered. Under the strain the Sioux were bewildered and frightened into hesitation and inaction.

On the last day of the struggle, with Chief Grass trying to control them, the Indians gave way to a fit of panic, rushed to the table and all but fought for a chance to touch the pen and have their names written as signatures to the official land sale papers. These were the warriors whose whirlwind assault had thrown back General Crook's strong column in June, 1876, and later that week had overwhelmed Custer's command.

Cheyenne village—
Little Wind River, Wyoming

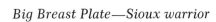

Big Breast Plate—Sioux warrior

Two Kettle Sioux Chief Long Mandan

The Mysterious Ride of Dr. Royer

On November 18, 1890, the town of Rushville, Nebraska, was startled by the sight of a buckboard stirring up a great cloud of dust behind a team at full gallop and white with lather. Above the clatter came the frantic shouts that the Sioux were rising and everybody would be murdered. The following day, the panic-crying Paul Revere, Dr. Royer, vastly incompetent new agent at the Pine Ridge Reservation, was back in that area under the protection of troops.

A few weeks earlier, edgy agent Royer had become alarmed by Indian activities he did not understand and had frightened white settlers, school and farm employees by ordering them to abandon their work and come to the safety of the reservation. Later he telegraphed the Indian Office that two hundred maddened ghost dancers had seized control of Pine Ridge and he must have soldiers at once. President Harrison commented leisurely and mildly that the agent should separate the friendly Indians from the ghost dancers and avoid any retaliatory action. Again agent Royer telegraphed and again Washington did nothing.

On ration day, November 17, thousands of Indians crowded the agency and Dr. Royer ordered the arrest of a ghost dancer named Little and his band closed in, threatening to kill all the whites. Chief American Horse restored order, the ghost dancers were induced to stand back and the police withdrew. When Dr. Royer returned to the agency after his frantic ride through Rushville, he was relieved to find several bodies of troops had arrived from several sources and the Indians gave him a new name—Young Man Afraid Of His Sioux.

Short Bull, the ghost dance prophet, had succeeded in stirring up band after band and into his camp came the followers of Two Strike, the Two Kettle tribesmen of Long Mandan (photo above) and others. Always wary and distrustful of U.S. troops, the Sioux rallied around Short Bull, who with his armed fanatics, moved westward to Pass Creek —a strategic victory march and one more blot against the ineptitude of government Indian policy.

Covered wagon train, 1882

*Crow Chief Iron Bull
and squaw*

*Photos (opp.)—Gardner, courtesy Smith-
sonian Inst., (top) Union Pacific R.R.,
(right) Smithsonian Inst.*

Little Shield—
Two views of famous Arapahoe chief

Arapahoe Chief Yellow Bear

Photos (top) U. of Wyoming, (left) Wyoming State Archives,
(opp.) Hiller, Smithsonian Inst.

Squaws curing robes and making buckskin

Arapahoe beaded moccasins

Shoshone sham battle

*Chief Runs Behind and
Joe Mood Joe—
Shoshone dancers*

Chief Washakie and his Shoshone warriors

The most famous chief of the Shoshones, peace maker, arbitrator and Moses of his people, was Washakie. He was born about 1798 in the upper Bitterroot Valley of Montana, his father being of Unadilla, Flathead and Shoshone stock and belonging to the Flathead tribe. According to family tradition he was killed when Washakie was five years old in a raid by the Blackfeet. The mother found refuge among the Lemhi Shoshones, her own people, on the Salmon River and here Washakie grew to manhood. He lived with a party of Bannocks for a few years, then joined the Shoshones of the Ft. Bridger country and spent the rest of his life— 1826 to 1832—among them. The name "Washakie" meant "The Rattler" or "Gourd Rattle."

Cheyenne warriors at a ford

Gros Ventres medicine lodge

Assiniboin Sioux village

Photos courtesy W. H. Over Museum

Chapter Twelve

BATTLE of SUMMIT SPRINGS

O<small>N THE DIVIDE</small> south of the South Platte River and about midway between old Fort Morgan and old Fort Sedgwick, opposite to which Julesburg now stands, there are some fine springs—the only good water in quite a region of territory. They are now called Summit Springs near the summit of a divide from which the water, when there is any, runs north and south.

In the winter of 1869, Major Frank North received orders to recruit his scouts for the summer campaign. He organized one company in February, and two the following April, the total number in the three companies being one hundred and fity men, exclusive of their white officers. In April General Carr took two of these companies and eight of the Fifth Cavalry, then stationed at Fort McPherson, to scout the country in the Republican, Solomon and Saline Valleys and their tributaries, and strike any marauding bands of Indians he might find.

At that time the Indians were raiding the advanced settlements of the Republican and Solomon, burning houses, killing and scalping men, women and children, and stealing all the horses they could find. When the third company of the scouts was organized Major North was ordered to take them across the country from Fort Kearny and join Gen. Carr's command at the mouth of Prairie Dog Creek in the Republican Valley.

After effecting this junction on the 5th of May, Major North scouted the country, returned to the Republican where he met a supply train sent out from Fort McPherson and proceeded up the valley. At the mouth of Medicine Creek the command struck the trail of a large Indian village and followed it up the river for one hundred and twenty-five miles. The trail then left the valley and bore off to the north until it struck Frenchman Creek, up that creek to its source, then over a divide to Summit Springs, about thirty-five miles from the headwaters of the Frenchman. The Indians of the village kept pickets out as a sort of rear guard but did not think of an attack from another quarter. The Pawnee scouts were constantly in the advance and kept the command well informed of the conditions and dispositions of the Indians. They had discovered the rear guard without being themselves seen and explained just how the attack should be made. A wide detour would have to be made and the village, encamped in a ravine near the springs, would have to be approached and attacked from the west. Every precaution was taken to conceal the movement of the troops.

The attack was made on the 11th of July. The heavy wagon train was left in the rear and the best horses and riders selected for the march, which was supposed to be, with the detour, at least fifty miles. The command arrived within about a mile and a half of the Indians undiscovered at about three o'clock p.m. but before the dispositions and arrangements for the final charge could be made, one company of cavalry unnecessarily exposed itself and this precipitated the attack. The Indians were Sioux, forty lodges, Chey-

Another account appearing in P<small>ACIFIC</small> T<small>OURIST</small>,
1879, by Henry T. Williams.

ennes, forty-five lodges—eighty-five in all. They had been in the raids together and were to separate the next day. They had evidently concluded to take one day at these splendid springs for the enjoyment of their farewell pow-wow but it proved to be a "bad medicine day" for them.

When they saw the exposed cavalry they ran out to gather in their horses which were quietly feeding a mile or more away. The troops and scouts charged down upon them with all speed, the former setting up their infernal war-whoop and going in with a headlong rush. The enemy was wholly unprepared for the attack, some of them quietly lounging in their tents. In fact it was nearly a complete surprise. They were all under the lead of Tall Bull, a noted Cheyenne chief and warrior, and numbered about five hundred men, women and children, nearly two hundred being warriors. Seventeen squaws and children were taken prisoners and as near as could be estimated, one hundred and sixty warriors were slain, among them Tall Bull. He was seen, as the troops approached, mounted upon his horse, with his wife and child behind him, trying to escape, but when he found his retreat cut off, he ran into a pocket or draw in the side of a ravine with almost perpendicular sides where some fifteen other warriors had taken refuge. He then took his wife and child and pushed them up on the bank of the pocket, telling her as he did this to go and give themselves up, perhaps their lives would be spared. The squaw and her child, a beautiful girl, went straight to Major North and, raising her hands in token of submission, drew them gently over his face and down his form to the ground where she sank upon her knees, her child standing beside her.

While Major North can talk Pawnee like a native he could not understand what she said but as all Indians use sign language to an extent he readily interpreted her motions to mean she surrendered and wanted him to spare their lives. He motioned her to rise which she did and motioned her to go a little way, sit down and stay there and she would not be harmed. She then by signs indicated there were seven living braves still in the pocket and asked him to go in after them, doubtless thinking that her husband might be saved with herself. He declined this request especially as the Indians were shooting everyone they could see from their concealed position, it being simply a question of life for life, and further told her that all the braves in the pocket would be killed. The troops and scouts stayed around the pocket until satisfied that there were no Indians living, and on entering found sixteen dead warriors and one dead squaw, one being Tall Bull.

In their raids in the Solomon Valley, they had captured two white women, whose lives they had spared for purposes worse than death, and at the time this attack was made, they were still alive. One of them had been taken by the principal Sioux chief and the other was appropriated by Tall Bull whose wife, doubtless from motives of ignorant jealousy, was accustomed to give her severe whippings at least six days out of every seven, and her body showed the marks where she had been severely bruised and lacerated. The Sioux chief's white captive, when he found she was likely to be rescued, was shot dead by him and only gasped for breath a few times when found by white officers. As near as could be learned her name was Susanna. It was afterwards ascertained that she was a Norwegian woman, and Gen. Carr in his report after the battle called the place Susanna Springs after this woman, near which she was decently buried, and which name they ought to bear now.

When the charge was first begun, Captain Cushing of the scouts, passing by the lodge of Tall Bull, entered it. The chief, as before stated, had fled with his wife and child, but in the lodge there remained the captive woman, whom he had shot and evidently left for dead. She was a German, unable to speak English, and up to this time, had supposed, from the presence of the scouts, that the fight was between Indians, and that whatever the result there would be no change for the better so far as she was concerned.

As the captain entered the lodge, he saw this woman in a sitting position, nearly denuded, with the blood running down her waist. When the chief left the tent, he had shot her in the side, aiming at her heart, but the bullet had struck a rib, glanced and

132

passed part way around her body, and came out near the spine. As the fight had just commenced, Capt. Cushing told her by motions and as best he could, to stay there and she would be taken care of, but not comprehending his meaning, and now for the first time realizing that white men were engaged in the battle, she thought as he left, that she was to be left, and with a pitiful moan, she lifted her arms, clasping him around his limbs, and in every possible way, begged him not to leave her with the savages. Others passing by, he called them in and the woman was partially made to understand she would be cared for. He disengaged himself from her embrace and after the fight had ended, returned and took her to the surgeon, who saw that her wounds were not fatal, that they were properly dressed and provided for her as best he could on the return march to Fort Sedgwick, where she was placed in the hospital and soon recovered.

A few months later, having no home or friends in the locality, she was married to a soldier who was discharged for reason of expiration of service. The troops and scouts captured in this fight nearly six hundred head of horses and mules, all the tents of the two tribes, an immense quantity of buffalo meats and robes, fifty guns of various kinds, with pistols, fancy Indian headdresses, trinkets etc. and $1,900 in twenty-dollar gold pieces, which the Indians had taken from this German woman's father at the time she was captured. About $900 of this gold was restored to the woman and if the white soldiers had been as honest and generous as the brave Pawnee scouts, when the appeal for its restoration was made, every lost dollar would have been returned.

Interior Crow Indian lodge

Cheyenne medicine tipi

decorated with spotted buffalo
head attached to snake's body

Assiniboin-Sioux camp

**Photos (opp.)—Curtis, courtesy Seattle Public Library,
(top) W. H. Over Museum, (bottom) U. of Wyoming**

Shoshone pipe

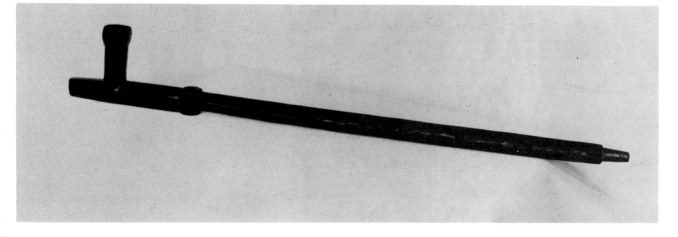

Taboonggwesha—Arapahoe

136

Windea—Arapahoe

Arapahoe boys

Chapter Thirteen

GRIM DAYS
with the INDIANS

THE INDIANS seemed unusually troublesome one year. Generally if they had the squaws and papooses with them they would not start any trouble, even though they might not be friendly.

I remember one morning when we were all at breakfast. It was an early, 6:00 o'clock breakfast too, and no one seemed very talkative. There was to be a busy day ahead, so we were eating a big breakfast of biscuits, potatoes, steak and coffee. Suddenly a rider came tearing into the yard. His horse was covered with lather. It was a neighbor. He jumped off and came in, but it was evident that he brought bad news. We all unconsciously arose from our chairs and benches. He dropped exhaustedly on a bench, and we gathered around him. This is what he told us.

In the middle of the night he had been awakened by a rider who came to his and Curley's cabin on the Upper Piney, bringing a tragic story. The rider was a trapper. His clothes were torn nearly off him. He was nearly starved, and his horse was almost dead. This fellow told our neighbor that he and his trapper partner had been trapping on Snake River, just above Gray's River. Fur was plentiful. They had built a crude cabin, planning on a fall and winter of lots of furs and a small amount of comfort. They had horses that had packed their crude equipment and they had been a great help. However, they were hard to catch. Fences were unheard of, so they used rope hobbles.

One morning the horses had strayed farther than usual, and since they had had a few days of rest after the cabin was finished, they were unusually hard to catch. They tore up the side of a hill about a mile from the cabin. The trapper who had left the cabin to catch the horses decided to try just once more. As he climbed the hill, he paused to look back at the cabin. Smoke was curling from the chimney. It was their home! Then, as he looked a second longer, he discerned a large group of riders and horses coming toward their cabin. They were Indians! There were squaws behind the bucks. He could even see the travois poles sticking up from the horses. He stood and watched them, thinking they were just going past. He felt no fear because the bucks, when they had the squaws with them, were generally peaceful, if not friendly. Furthermore, neither he nor his trapper friend had ever had the slightest trouble with any Indians. Being rather tired, he kept on watching, and as he did, he could see Jack, his partner, come out of the cabin. Jack's hat was on the back of his head, a sign of western nonchalance.

Written by Mrs. Helen Sargent, "Incidents in the Life of Norris Griggs" in ANNALS OF WYOMING, *Vol. 25, January 1953, No. 1.*

Sioux camp

It was customary for a war party to ride in circles around the tipi of a chief before setting out on a raid into enemy country.

Photo—Curtis, Seattle Public Library

Some Indians pushed ahead of the others, but talk was difficult, and as they were trying to convey ideas, other Indians gathered closer. Suddenly he could see one of the bucks wave his arms, and on a high lope, he and his horse tore completely around the cabin. This seemed strange. Then as the racing Indian came back to his comrades, he knocked Jack's hat to the ground. At this the Indians seemed to be readying their horses, and he could hear their weird voices. Jack seemed to try to get back into the cabin.

Then suddenly one buck rode up to him and grabbed Jack around the neck. Partly dragging and partly pulling, the Indian started toward the rest of the group. Another buck grabbed Jack's legs and in some way they threw him across the front of a horse. The Indians yipped and yelled; some of them rode in a fantastic circle. No one will ever know what the whole thing was about or why, but the onlooker stood spellbound, hanging to a large rock. He could not believe that the Indians meant harm as the squaws seemed to be taking part. Soon all rode off toward the Snake River. (The cabin was situated on a little bench. The river made a bend and there was a small piece of land near that was a natural meadow.) He could see them go straight to the river, and as they neared it they hurried faster. The rider carrying Jack led the group but stopped his horse at the bank of the stream. Several bucks then arrived and yelling, jumped from their horses and grabbed Jack. Then they threw him into the river. The amazed watcher could not believe what he saw. Before he could move, one buck jumped into the river, grabbed Jack as he came up, and dragged him to the bank. He thought, or really tried to think, that this was just a game—an Indian way of having fun. Ten or more of them were still at the cabin. Then with a big yell the Indians at the bank again siezed Jack and threw him into the river. One big fellow jumped in, and as Jack came to the surface, this buck pushed him in again. By this time the watcher's curiosity had turned to fear. This was no game. He looked for his horses. Could he catch one? Should he go back to the cabin with that milling band of Indians? He had no gun, and even if he had, would he be able to stand alone against so many?

As he looked again at the river scene, he could see them dragging Jack out once more. Then they shook him and helped him up. At this the watcher decided to catch a horse and go for help. Help? Where could he find any help! The soldiers at Ft. Washakie and Ft. Hall were supposed to keep the Indians under control. He had heard of the settlement on Big Piney, the ferry across the Green River, and a trail over the mountains. This seemed the closest way to help.

He couldn't understand why the Indians hadn't seen him or the two horses. With one more glance at the river he was sickened with the sight. They were throwing Jack in again. One buck was standing by to hold him under. He made a dash for the horse, and for some reason the Indians didn't see him. He caught one horse, frantically took off the rope hobbles, and made a rope halter from them. When he was ready to mount, he looked once more toward the river, and as he did so, poor Jack was again being pulled out. This time he was completely limp, and the Indians were kicking him. With a wild, desperate leap the trapper got on the horse and crept over the ridge. As he did so, one last glance at the cabin told him the cabin was in flames.

Just ahead was Spring Creek leading straight east and in that direction lay Big Piney and Ft. Washakie. He urged the horse on and on; up and up, and was very grateful when he found the dim trail. He traveled until it was too dark to see, then he lay down, exhausted from his ride. He slept a few hours, but as the nights in August are short, he was up at the crack of dawn and on his way again. He followed the trail to the source of a fair-sized stream that was running in the right direction.

At last he came to a bench. The water had cut through and he could see a cabin in the distance. His body ached. He had had no food but some berries that he had hardly had time to pick. After what seemed ages he came to the cabin. There he found two cowboys outfitted to gather beef. They gave him food, he rested a bit and told his story. His one object was to notify the soldiers at Ft. Washakie of this tragic and uncalled-for Indian affair, and have the Indians punished. He also hoped to gather a posse on Big Piney to help catch them as they went back to the fort.

My neighbor told us all this as we stood around horrified. He said that Curley, his partner, had gone with the word to Ft. Washakie, and that he and the trapper were gathering a posse to pursue the Indians. It seemed probably that they would circle north, and perhaps they would go over Union Pass to the fort.

Well, we all looked at each other, and finally Mr. McKay said, "Half of us will go, half of us will stay on the ranch."

I surely wanted to go and was delighted when he pointed to me. In a few minutes we were on our horses, and with our guns at our sides we rode off to meet the rest of the posse at the ferry just above the Mule Shoe. We were to make a circle toward Upper Green River and attempt to get in ahead of the Indians as they went to the fort.

When we got to the ferry there were five or six men waiting for us. There were eight in all. We rode hard and fast, watching each trail for signs, and scanning the horizon constantly. At last we rode up on a high bench and from there could see a group of twelve or fifteen riders, but they weren't moving. We knew that there would be about twenty Indians in the bunch that we were looking for, so this puzzled us. As we rode nearer we could see that these men were soldiers, so we whipped up our horses. When we got there a grizzly sight met our eyes. There on the ground, scattered about, lay twenty dead Indians and many dead horses. There were also about eight or nine dead papooses — all shot by the soldiers who had beaten us there by twenty minutes. Thus was avenged the unwarranted murder of the white trapper.

We took what we wanted from the dead Indians, and headed home. I took some buckskin, some blankets, and an Indian packsaddle. This had a large, odd horn in front and back. I also took a needle gun. It was a single shot, four-inch shell, breech load, pulled back like a bolt action, had a firing pin. I prized this gun highly, but have no idea of what became of it as the years went on.

Pioneer's ox yoke

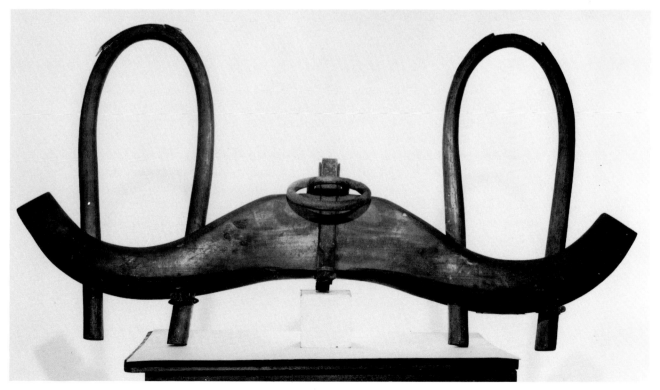

Cheyennes and buffalo hide tipis

"Trader Alonzo Simms bought many buffalo robes from the Cheyennes for a dollar or a dollar and a half each," wrote Henry T. Williams in the *Pacific Tourist*. "The Indian bucks of course would trade them gladly for whiskey, then beat the squaws for not hurrying with the work. For they did all of it. They cut the skins from the dead animals, slain by the braves, stretched and dried them flesh up.

"With a piece of sharpened bone or iron, two inches long on the edge, which was tied to a piece of elk thigh bone and used like a garden hoe, a squaw would work for hours, scraping off the flesh and reducing the hide to an even thickness. Then she would cover it with an unholy mixture of lard, soap and salt or, if she had them, buffalo brains which were always preferable. The hide would then be rolled up and laid by for two or three days.

"After stretching it out in the frame again, the treated side to the sun, the squaw would scrape it dry with a dull knife or her bone or iron implement. It was then taken up, drawn across a rope, flesh side to the rope, until it was thoroughly soft and pliant."

Photos (above) courtesy Nebraska State Hist. Soc.,
(opp.) Curtis, Seattle Public Library

Sioux winter camp

Samuel Lone Bear

Son and daughter of chief.

Alice Lone Bear

Photos (top, left and opp.) courtesy U. of Wyoming,
(top right) Pettigrew Museum

Sioux Chief Lone Bear

Death of Lone Bear

The upper waters of the Republican River, where the states of Kansas, Colorado and Nebraska come together, abounded with buffalo and was a favorite Indian camping ground. It was in this area, in the early summer of 1869, the Cheyenne Lone Bear was killed in a skirmish with Pawnee troops of Major Frank North. Scout William Cody was in this command.

Cheyenne women and children were fleeing on horse and foot before the approach of some twenty-five or thirty Pawnees. From a hill four Cheyenne braves—Two Crows, Plenty of Bull Meat, Pile of Bones and Lone Bear (photo opposite page)—who had good horses and were prepared to fight, saw a woman on a horse going very slowly. Lone Bear called to the other warriors: "We must stop here and fight for this woman. We will stay behind and fight these people off."

Three Pawnees were close to the woman and shooting at her. Two Crows and Plenty of Bull Meat rode down to her, whipped her horse and turned it up into the hills, the three Pawnees riding back to their main body. The two Cheyennes rode up the rise to find Lone Bear and Pile of Bones on the ground, shot off their horses and a number of Pawnees scalping them and throwing their war bonnets in the air.

This incident was one of the early events of the Battle of Summit Springs in which Chief Tall Bull and fifty other Cheyennes were killed when Major North's Pawnees annihilated the Indian village, capturing eighteen women and children and taking some four hundred horses and mules.

*Capt. Sanderson's camp at the
ford while gathering bones*

*Bones gathered after
Custer Massacre*

Chapter Fourteen

A RIDE for LINIMENT and LIFE

I JUST DON'T RECALL the year, but it was while I was working for Amos Smith—must have been the spring of 1885 or 1886 that a baby was born to our neighbor and part-time hand — Walt Nickels. Walt lived on his own place and worked for Amos when he was needed or could. The baby was fine, so was Walt, but the mother, Anne, was not doing so well. This gave us all great concern. It seemed she had developed milk leg, or as it is called today, phlebitis. All the neighbors responded not only with their help but their remedies. But Anne did not seem to improve. At last some one thought if only we had some of Uncle Johnny's liniment!

Now Uncle Johnny Zimmers peddled medicine, trapped and bought furs, and prospected on the side. He had been a druggist before he came to this country, and just prior to coming here had been a scout in Johnston's Army. He had some horses, and Mr. Smith took care of them for him. Uncle Johnny was a good trapper, but he was perhaps best known for his liniment. I believe it had four ingredients—two of them I cannot remember—but eggs and ammonia were the other two. When he could not get hens eggs, he used sage chicken eggs. It was real white, and most everyone would vouch for its effectiveness when it came to bruises, sprains, rheumatism, or any inflammation.

I was elected to go find Uncle Johnny and get the liniment. All we knew was that he was going up the Indian trail which went through Snider Basin over to the Blackfoot Reservation, and that he had said that if that trail did not look good for trapping he would drop over on to Cottonwood or Horse Creek or Beaver. I had a colt, pretty skittish and black as coal, which sure needed riding, so we were soon on our way.

I went up Piney where the Ralph Mills place now is, and there I ran into Le Viae. I asked about Uncle Johnny, and he told me he had passed him and that he was headed for Cottonwood. This Le Viae was an old squaw man. He followed the mess wagons or game. He bought or begged hides—even the entrails. His squaws made gloves from the hides and sold them for fifty cents. (They called the 50-cent piece a little dollar, and the dollar the big dollar.) Le Viae wanted me to go with him; said that I could have the pick of his squaws if I would. But I didn't care for any squaws and I had liniment to get.

So I crossed over to Cottonwood. About five that evening I found Uncle Johnny on a branch of Upper Cottonwood. He fixed me the liniment, but said I had better stay with him that night. He had heard there was a band of Shoshones in that vicinity, sorta on the war path. I decided to stay, and so picketed my horse. We had supper and I noticed that Uncle Johnny fixed his bed in between willows—almost surrounded by willows. We sat by a little camp fire and talked for quite a while, and finally Uncle Johnny said we had better roll in. I noticed, as I crawled in with him, that he put his needle gun in along side of him.

Written by Mrs. Helen Sargent, "Incidents in the Life of Norris Griggs" in ANNALS OF WYOMING, *Vol. 25, January 1953, No. 1.*

I had my .44 on my saddle but I didn't think anything about it. We talked a little while, then I went to sleep.

I don't know how long I had been asleep when "Bang!" went Uncle Johnny's gun. I jumped out of bed sure the Indians had us, but there was nothing in sight except Uncle Johnny, holding his still-smoking gun. Now no one ever heard Uncle Johnny swear. The worst he ever said was "Confound." But this time he said: "Confound, that was bad luck, but I guess I've got our meat."

By this time Uncle Johnny was up, and I followed him around the willows, and there, sure enough, was an Indian buck, hit between the eyes. That needle gun shot such a slug that it really had torn the top of his head right off. Uncle Johnny had seen the Indian through the willows, and his shot, as he said, was bad luck, not only for the Indian. 'Twasn't the first one, but he just wasn't proud to kill one, and felt that it didn't do him any good. The Indian had a gun in his hand—it was either him or us.

I said, "What are we going to do with him, bury him?" Uncle Johnny said, "No, we're throwing him in the creek." We did.

Then Uncle Johnny said he was packing up and getting out of there, and I could go with him or not, just as I liked. He was going north, so I decided I too would get out of there, but I went south. My horse rested some and in no time we were burning the ground getting out of there. I just let that horse go for all he was worth. I had the bottle of liniment in my pocket, and it was up to us to get it there.

We headed down creek and arrived before daylight at Frank Ball's place. By noon that day I was back at the ranch with the liniment. The mother recovered. Later the Nickels moved over into the Lander country where Anne died. Walt came back to Piney —had a store there. . . .

Shoshone prayer horns

Cheyenne camp

Cheyenne women in camp

*Cheyennes in
solitary camp*

*Cheyenne camp with
hides drying*

Cheyenne camp

in cottonwoods along
Tongue River, Montana

Shoshone war chief's tent

Chief Iron Crow—Shoshone

Has No Horse—Shoshone

Photos courtesy Union Pacific R. R., (opp.) U. of Wyoming

Spotted Tail—Brule Sioux Chief   *Spotted Tail's wife*

Photos courtesy Nebraska State Hist. Soc.

Murder of Spotted Tail

At the height of his career in 1878, Spotted Tail was head chief of the Brule Sioux and looked upon as a great leader by all divisions of the Sioux and whites as well. Due to his efforts many hostile Sioux tribes had surrendered to the military at the agencies and in recognition of this, officials at Washington had made him an "honorary officer" in the U.S. Army with pay for life. The plan ended in talk mainly because Spotted Tail did not abide by Indian Bureau policy of trying to make farmers out of free-spirited Sioux hunters and warriors.

During the winter of 1880-81 a plot was set in motion to assassinate the head chief. Having lost his place as police chief on the Rosebud Reservation, Crow Dog bitterly blamed Spotted Tail. He was reduced to selling firewood—cut by his wife—at the agency.

Chief Spotted Tail was living in his own camp north of the agency with separate tipis for his four wives and their children. Early in 1881 he "stole" the young and handsome wife of a Brule warrior. He did not drink or smoke but could not resist pretty girls. Legend has it that resentment over the acquisition of the girl caused Crow Dog's anger, but facts disprove this.

After the tribal count and feast on August 5, 1881, Spotted Tail mounted his pony and started home. Crow Dog's wagon approached with his wife seated beside him. He jumped to the ground and bent as though to tie his moccasin thong, but when he raised up he was holding a gun and shot Spotted Tail through the left breast. The chief fell from his pony but immediately got up and tried to draw his pistol, reeling over backward and falling dead. Brought to trial in Deadwood in 1882, Crow Dog was sentenced to hang but was later reprieved by order of the Supreme Court as having taken the life by tribal custom and was not subject to laws governing United States citizens.

Chapter Fifteen

INDIAN
RETRIBUTION

I T WAS IN the summer of 1882 or 1883 that we had some trouble with the Indians at the mouth of Beaver. At this time many cattle were ranging there until fall, but in the past year they had scattered far from Beaver, and they were anything but fat. The cattlemen figured this was because the Indians gathered on Beaver for the summer. They came from the east and the west, and their tepees covered the landscape as far as one could see, from the mouth of Beaver up. They hunted the antelope, and had many games, mainly horse races. As a result the cattle suffered.

It was decided to see the Indians and see what could be done to remedy the situation. A group of men including McKay, Swan, Liefer, Charles Ackels, a New York boy, Tom Smith, and myself rode to the Indian camp. There we found the chiefs, and McKay and Swan were elected to do the talking.

While they were busy, we looked the outfit over. Certainly there were lots of tepees and many horses. That day they were having races. There was quite a clearing. It was not too wide, but it was nearly a mile and a half long. They seemed to be having a big time that afternoon. Each Indian would bet on his horse without saddle or rider. When they were ready for the race a young boy nine or ten years old was put on each horse. Usually not more than two contestants raced at one time.

By the time the race was ready to start, there would be Indians with long willows stationed along the clearing at various intervals. The race began, and as a horse passed each station he was whipped by those interested in seeing him win. I noticed an old Indian who seemed to have a ring-side seat, or at least he thought he had. He was just about half way up the length of the clearing. He just sat there with the racing horses going by on either side of him. There was a great deal of yelling by the Indians as they vigorously took sides in the race. The boys rode their horses as if they were glued to them.

As we watched, Charles Ackels made the remark that he would bet that the little buckskin horse he was riding could outrun any of the Indian horses he had seen.

By this time Mr. McKay and Mr. Swan came back to us, and they didn't look very happy as the Indians had said that if they had to move from this place they would get even with us. That was always a bad situation.

Just then another race was finished, and as we watched one of us told Mr. McKay and Swan how Ackels had boasted that his buckskin could outrun any horse that he had seen there. That just suited McKay and Swan, who immediately told the chiefs, and as such a race was just to the Indians' liking, they gathered around and asked, "Which horse?" as we pointed to the buckskin. They took us up, and the bets were on. We threw in our 44's and chaps against a pile of beaver skins, buckskin gloves, and blankets. They

Written by Mrs. Helen Sargent, "Incidents in the Life of Norris Griggs" in ANNALS OF WYOMING, *Vol. 25, January 1953, No. 1.*

didn't want money, but how they did want chaps and guns! We first threw in one 44, and then they threw in their bet. Then we added another, and they added another, until we had all we could bet in the pile, and with their hides, blankets, and gloves, what a huge pile it was! There was a little secret about this buckskin horse that the Indians didn't know —he was scared to death of Indians.

While the bet was being arranged to the satisfaction of both parties, Ackels ran his horse across the clearing once just to try it out. Then everything was ready. The Indians had their horse and boy all set. The whipper-uppers were all in place, and the starting signal was given. The Indians in their zeal started whipping their horse, and it was off ahead of Ackels' whose buckskin had a man as well as a heavy saddle to carry. When the Indians saw their horse leading how they did whoop and yell, and we thought: "There goes our guns and chaps." However, by the time Buckskin got to the center of the clearing, that old Indian sitting there rose up. Buckskin took one look at him and let loose with an unbelievable spurt of speed. He won by a length, and it was our turn to whoop and yell. The Indians wanted to run the race over, but we didn't. We grabbed our winnings in a hurry, packed up, donned our chaps and guns, and rode on to Frank Ball's that night. (At this time he had just moved to Cottonwood.)

The race didn't improve the feelings of the Indians, and to be ordered off Beaver was bad. They took willows, set them afire, and riding their horses, they dragged the burning willows back and forth through the deep grass until they had set the whole country afire. It burned to Green River, and in places the fire crossed over the Rim. It burned for a week and this was Indian vengeance.

Sioux woman in mourning, about 1884

Photos courtesy Nebraska State Hist. Soc., (opp.) Wyoming State Archives

Sioux burial on poles

*Shoshone woman
on the move*

Sioux girl

Photos (top and left) courtesy Nebraska State Hist. Soc., (right) Wyoming State Archives

Little Big Man—Oglala Sioux

Charges Two—Sioux

Chapter Sixteen

MY LAST BUFFALO HUNT

AMONG ALL the glowing and glorious autumns of the forty-odd which I have enjoyed in clear-skied Nebraska, the most delicious, dreamy, and tranquil was that of 1861. The first day of October in that year surpassed in purity of air, clouds, and coloring all the other October days in my whole life. The prairies were not a somber brown, but a gorgeous old-gold; and there drifted in the dry, crisp atmosphere lace-like fragments of opalescent clouds which later in the afternoon gave the horizon the look of a far-away ocean upon which one could see fairy ships, and upon its farther-away shores splendid castles, their minarets and towers tipped with gold. The indolence of savagery saturated every inhalation, and all physical exertion except in the hunt or chase seemed repellant, irksome, and unendurable.

Then it was that—like an evolution from environment—the desire and impulse to go upon a buffalo hunt seized upon and held and encompassed and dominated every fibre of my physical, every ambition and aspiration of my mental, make-up. Controlled by this spontaneous reincarnation of the barbaric tastes and habits of some nomadic ancestor of a prehistoric generation, arrangements for an excursion to Fort Kearny on the Platte (Colonel Alexander, of the regular army, then in command) were completed. With food rations, tent and camping furniture, and arms and ammunition, and pipes and tobacco, and a few drops of distilled rye (to be used only when snakebitten), a light one-horse wagon drawn by a well-bred horse which was driven by the writer, was early the next morning leaving Arbor Lodge, and briskly speeding westward on the "Overland Trail" leading to California. And what rare roads there were in those buoyant days of the pioneers! All the prairies, clear across the plains from the Missouri river to the mountains, were perfectly paved with solid, tough, but elastic sod. And no asphalt or block-paved avenue or well-worked pike can give the responsive pressure to the touch of a human foot or a horse-hoof that came always from those smooth and comely trails. Especially in riding on horseback were the felicities of those primitive prairie roads emphasized and accentuated. Upon them one felt the magnetism and life of his horse; they animated and electrified him with the vigor and spirit of the animal until in elation, the rider became, at least emotionally, a centaur—a semi-horse human. The invigoration and exaltation of careering over undulating prairies on a beautiful, speedy, and spirited horse thrilled every sense and satisfied, as to exhilaration, by physical exercise, the entire mental personality. Nature's roads in Nebraska are unequaled by any of their successors.

This excursion was in a wagon without springs; and after driving alone, as far as the Weeping Water crossing, I overtook an ox train loaded with goods and supplies for Gilman's ranch on the Platte away beyond Fort Kearny.

One of the proprietors, Mr. Jed Gilman, was in command of the outfit, and by his cordial and hospitable invitation I became his willing and voracious guest for the noon-

This paper by J. Sterling Morton, was included in NEBRASKA PIONEER REMINISCENCES, *Nebraska Society of Daughters of the American Revolution.*

day meal. With a township for a dining room over which arched the turquoise-colored sky, like a vaulted ceiling, frescoed with clouds of fleecy white, we sat down upon our buffalo robes to partake of a hearty meal. There was no white settler within miles of our camp. The cry of "Dinner is now ready in the next car" had never been heard west of the Mississippi river nor even dreamed of in the East. The bill of fare was substantial: bacon fried, hot bread, strong coffee, stronger raw onions, and roasted potatoes. And the appetite which made all exquisitely palatable and delicious descended to us out of the pure air and the exhilaration of perfect health. And then came the post-prandial pipe— how fragrant and solacing its fumes—from Virginia natural leaf, compared to which the exhalations from a perfecto cigar are today a disagreeable stench. There was then the leisure to smoke, the liberty and impulse to sing, to whoop, and to generally simulate the savages into whose hunting grounds we were making an excursion. Life lengthened out before us like the Overland route to the Pacific in undulations of continuously rising hillocks and from the summit of each one scaled we saw a similarly attractive one beyond in a seemingly never-ending pathway of pleasure, ambition, and satisfaction. The gold of the Pacific coast was not more real then than the invisible possibilities of life, prosperity, success, and contentment which were to teem, thrive, and abound upon those prairies which seemed only farms asleep or like thoughts unuttered—books unopened.

But the smoke over, the oxen again yoked to the wagons and the train, like a file of huge white beetles, lumbered along to the songs, swearing, and whip-crackings of the drivers toward the crossing of Salt creek. However, by my persuasive insistence, Mr. Gilman left his wagon boss in charge and getting into my wagon accompanied me. Together we traveled briskly until quite late at night when we made camp at a point near where the town of Wahoo now stands. There was a rough ranch cabin there, and we remained until the following morning, when we struck out at a brisk trot toward Fort Kearny, entering the Platte Valley at McCabe's ranch. The day and the road were perfect. We made good time. At night we were entertained at Warfield's, on the Platte. The water in the well there was too highly flavored to be refreshing. Nine skunks had been lifted out of it the day of our arrival and only Platte river water could be had, which we found rather stale for having been hauled some distance in an old sorghum cask. But fatigue and a square meal are an innocent opiate and we were soon fast asleep under the open sky with the moon and stars only to hear how loudly a big ranchman can snore in a bedroom of a million or more acres. In the morning of our third day out, we were up, breakfasted with the sunrise, and drove on over the then untried railroad bed of the Platte Valley at a rattling gait. The staunch and speedy animal over which the reins were drawn, a splendid bay of gentle birth, had courage and endurance by heredity, and thus we made time. Ranches were from twenty to thirty miles apart. And the night of the third day found us at Mabin's.

This was a hotel, feed barn, dry goods establishment, and saloon all under one roof, about thirty miles from Fort Kearny. After a reasonably edible supper, Mr. Gilman and I were escorted to the saloon and informed that we could repose and possibly sleep in the aisle which divided it from the granary which was filled with oats. Our blankets and buffalo robes were soon spread out in this narrow pathway. On our right were about two hundred bushels of oats in bulk, and on our left the counter which stood before variously shaped bottles containing alleged gins, supposed whiskey, and probable brandy. We had not been long in a recumbent position before—instead of sleep gently creeping over us— we experienced that we were race courses and grazing grounds for innumerable myriads of sand fleas. Immediately Gilman insisted that we should change our apartment and go out on the prairies near a haystack; but I stubbornly insisted that, as the fleas had not bitten me, I would continue indoors. Thereupon Gilman incontinently left, and then the fleas with vicious vigor and voracity assaulted me. The bites were sharp, they were incisive and decisive. They came in volleys. Then in wrath I too arose from the lowly but lively couch between the oats and the bar and sullenly went out under the starlit sky to find Mr. Gilman energetically whipping his shirt over a wagon wheel to disinfest it from fleas. But the sand fleas of the Platte are not easily discharged or diverted, from a fair and juicy victim. They have a wonderful tenacity of purpose. They trotted and hopped and skipped along behind us to the haystack. They affectionately and fervidly abided with us on the prairie; and it is safe to say that there never were two human beings more thoroughly perforated, more persistently punctured with flea bites than were the two guests at Mabin's ranch during all the long and agonizing night. However, there came an end to the darkness and the attempt at sleep, and after an early breakfast we resumed the Fort Kearny journey to arrive at its end in the late afternoon of the fourth day.

There I found Colonel Alexander, of the regulary army, in command. John Heth, of Virginia, was the sutler for the post and after some consultation and advisement it was determined that we might without much danger from Indians go south to the Republican river for a buffalo hunt. At that time the Cheyennes, who were a bloodthirsty tribe, were in arms against the white people and yearning for their scalps wherever found. But to avoid or mitigate dangers Colonel Alexander considerately detailed Lieutenant Bush with twelve enlisted men, all soldiers of experience in the Indian country, to go with us to the Republican Valley as an escort or guard—in military parlance, on detached service. Thus our party moved southward with ample force of arms for its defense.

The four hunters of the expedition were Lieutenant Bush, John Heth, John Talbot (who had been honorably discharged from the regular army after some years of service) and myself. The excursion was massed and ready for departure at 8 o'clock on the bright morning of October 6, 1861. The course taken was nearly due south from the present site of Kearney city in Buffalo county. The expedition consisted of two large army wagons, four mules attached to each wagon, a light, two-horse spring wagon', and four trained riding horses experienced in the chase, together with twelve soldiers of the regular U. S. army and the gentlemen already named. It had not traveled more than twenty-five miles south of Fort Kearny before it came in view of an immense herd of buffalo.

My first sight of these primitive beeves of the plains I shall never forget. They were so distant that I could not make out their individual forms and I at once jumped to the conclusion that they were only an innumerable lot of crows sitting about upon the knobs and hillocks of the prairies. But in a few moments, when we came nearer, they materialized and were, sure enough, real bellowing, snorting, wallowing buffaloes. At first they appeared to give no heed to our outfit, but after we saddled and mounted our horses and rode into their midst they began to scatter and to form into small bands, single file. The herd separated into long, black swaying strings and each string was headed by the best meat among its numbers. The leading animal was generally a three-year-old cow. Each of these strings, or single-file bands, ran in a general southeast direction and each of the four hunters—Bush, Heth, Talbot, and the writer—selected a string and went for the preeminent animal with enthusiasm, zeal, and impulsive foolhardiness.

In the beginning of the pell-mell, hurry-scurry race it seemed that it would be very easy to speedily overtake the desired individual buffalo that we intended to shoot and kill. The whole band seemed to run leisurely. They made a sort of sidewise gait, a movement such as one often sees in a dog running ahead of a wagon on a country road. Upon the level prairie we made very perceptible gains upon them, but when a declivity was reached and we made a down hill gallop we were obliged to rein in and hold up the horses, or take the chances of a broken leg or neck by being ditched in a badger or wolf hole. But the buffaloes with their heavy shoulders and huge hair-matted heads lumbered along down the incline with great celerity, gaining so much upon us that every now and then one of them would drop out from the line upon reaching an attractive depression, roll over two or three times in his "wallow," jump up and join his fleeing fellows before we could reach him.

But finally after swinging and swaying hither and thither with the band or line as it swayed and swung, the lead animal was reached and with much exultation and six very nervous shots put to death. My trophy proved to be a buffalo cow of two or three years

161

of age; and after she had dropped to the ground, a nimble calf, about three months old, evidently her progeny, began making circles around and around the dead mother and bleating pitifully, enlarging the circle each time, until at last it went out of sight onto the prairie and alone, all the other parts of the herd having scattered beyond the rising bluffs.

That afternoon was fuller of tense excitement, savage enthusiasms, zeal and barbaric ambition than any other that could be assorted from my life of more than sixty years. There was a certain amount of ancestral heathenism aroused in every man, spurring a horse to greater swiftness, in that chase for large game. And there was imperial exultation of the primitive barbaric instinct when the game fell dead and its whooping captors surrounded its breathless carcass.

But the wastefulness of the buffalo hunter of those days was wicked beyond description and, because of its utter recklessness of the future, wholly unpardonable. Only the hump, ribs, the tongue, and perhaps now and then one hind-quarter were saved for use from each animal. The average number of pounds of meat saved from each buffalo killed between the years 1860 and 1870 would not exceed twenty. In truth, thousands of buffaloes were killed merely to get their tongues and pelts. The inexcusable and unnecessary extermination of those beef-producing and very valuable fur-bearing animals only illustrates the extravagance of thoughtlessness and mental nearsightedness in the American people when dealing with practical and far-reaching questions. It also demonstrates, in some degree, the incapacity of the ordinary every-day law-makers of the United States. Game laws have seldom been enacted in any of the states before the virtual extinction of the game they purposed to protect. Here in Nebraska among big game were many hundreds of thousands of buffaloes, tens of thousands of elk and deer and antelope, while among smaller game the wild turkey and the prairie chicken were innumerable. But today Nebraska game is practically extinct. Even the prairie chicken and the wild turkey are seldom found anywhere along the Missouri bluffs in the southern and eastern part of the commonwealth.

Looking back: what might have been accomplished for the conservation of game in the trans-Missouri country is suggested so forcibly that one wonders at the stupendous stupidity which indolently permitted its destruction.

The first night outward and southeastward from Fort Kearny we came to Turkey creek which empties into the Republican river. There, after dark, tents were pitched at a point near the place where the government in previous years established kilns and burned lime for the use of soldiers in building quarters for themselves and the officers at Fort Kearny which was constructed in 1847 by Stewart L. Van Vliet, now a retired brigadier general and the oldest living graduate of West Point. After a sumptuous feast of buffalo steak, a strong pint of black coffee and a few pipes of good tobacco, our party retired; sleep came with celerity and the camp was peacefully at rest, with the exception of two regular soldiers who stood guard until 12 o'clock, and were then relieved by two others who kept vigil until sunrise. At intervals I awoke during the night and listened to the industrious beavers building dams on the creek. They were shoveling mud with their trowel-shaped tails into the crevices of their dams with a constantly-resounding slapping and splashing all night. The architecture of the beaver is not unlike that which follows him and exalts itself in the chinked and daubed cabins of the pioneers.

The darkness was followed by a dawn of beauty and breakfast came soon thereafter, and for the first time my eyes looked out upon the attractive, fertile and beautiful valley of the Republican river. All that delightful and invigorating day we zealously hunted. We found occasionally small bands of buffaloes here and there among the bluffs and hills along the valley of the Republican. But these animals were generally aged and of inferior quality. Besides such hunting, we found a great quantity of blue-winged and green-winged teal in the waters of the Republican and bagged not a few of them. There is no water-fowl, in my judgment, not even the redheaded duck and canvasback duck, which excels in delicate tissue and flavor the delicious teal.

Just a little before sundown, on the third day of our encampment, by the bluffs land of the Republican, Lieutenant Bush and Mr. Heth in one party, and John Talbot and I in another, were exploring the steep, wooded bluffs which skirted the valley. The timber growing at that time on the sides of these bluffs was, much of it, of very good size and I shall never forget going down a precipitous path along the face of a hill and suddenly coming upon a strange and ghastly sight among the top limbs and branches of an oak tree which sprang from the rich soil of a lower level. The weird object which then impressed itself upon my memory forever was a dead Indian sitting upright in a sort of wicker-work coffin which was secured by thongs to the main trunk of the tree. The robe with which he had been clothed had been torn away by buzzards and only the denuded skeleton sat there. The bleached skull leered and grinned at me as though the savage instinct to repulse an intruder from their hunting grounds still lingered in the fleshless head. Perfectly I recall the long scalp-lock, floating in the wind, and the sense of dread and repellant fear which, for the startled moment, took possession of me in the presence of this arborially interred Indian whose remains had been stored away in a tree-top instead of having been buried in the ground.

Not long after this incident we four came together again down in the valley at a great plum orchard. The plum trees covered an area of several acres; they stood exceedingly close together. The frosts had been just severe enough to drop the fruit onto the ground. Never before nor since have my eyes beheld or my palate tasted as luscious fruit as those large yellow and red plums which were found that afternoon lying in bushels in the valley of the Republican. While we were all seated upon the ground eating plums and praising their succulence and flavor we heard the click-cluck of a turkey. Immediately we laid ourselves flat upon the earth and in the course of ten minutes beheld a procession of at least seventy-five wild turkeys feeding upon plums. We remained moveless and noiseless until those turkeys had flown up into the tall cottonwood trees standing thereabouts and gone to roost. Then after darkness had settled down upon the face of the earth we faintly discerned the black forms or hummocks of fat turkeys all through the large and leafless limbs of the cottonwoods which had been nearly defoliated by the early frosts of October. It required no deft markmanship or superior skill to bring down forty of those birds in a single evening. That number we took into camp. In quick time we had turkey roasted, turkey grilled, turkey broiled; and never have I since eaten any turkey so well flavored, so juicy and rich, as that fattened upon the wild plums of the Republican Valley in the year 1861.

At last, surfeited with hunting and its successes, we set out on our return to Fort Kearny. When about half way across the divide, a sergeant, one of the most experienced soldiers and plainsmen of the party, declared that he saw a small curl of smoke in the hazy distance and a little to the west and south of us. To my untrained eye the smoke was at first invisible, but with a field glass I ultimately discerned a delicate little blue thread hanging in the sky, which the soldiers pronounced smoke ascending from an Indian camp. Readjusting the glasses I soon made out to see three Indians stretched by the fire seemingly asleep, while two were sitting by the embers apparently cooking, eating and drinking. Very soon, however, the two feasters espied our wagons and party. Immediately they came running on foot to meet us; the other three, awaking, followed them; speedily they were in our midst. They proved, however, to be peaceful Pawnees. Mr. John Heth spoke the language of that tribe and I shall never forget the coolness with which these representatives of that nomadic race informed him that Mrs. Heth and his little two-years-of-age daughter, Minnie, were in good health in their wigwam at Fort Kearny; they were sure of it because they had looked into the window of the Heth home the day before and saw them eating and drinking their noonday meal.

These Indians then expressed a wish for some turkey feathers. They were told to help themselves. Immediately they pulled out a vast number of the large feathers of the wings and tails and decorated their own heads with them. The leader of the aboriginal ex-

163

pedition, in conversation with Mr. Heth, informed him that although they were on foot they carried the lariats which we saw hanging from their arms for the purpose of hitching onto and annexing some Cheyenne ponies which they were going south to steal. They walked away from home, but intended to ride back. The barbaric commander in charge of this larcenous expedition was named "The Fox," and when questioned by Mr. Heth as to the danger of the enterprise, and informed that he might probably lose his life and get no ponies at all, Captain Fox smiled and said grimly that he knew he should ride back to the Pawnee village on the Loup the owner of good horses; that only a year or two before that time he had been alone down into the Cheyenne village and got a great many horses safely out and up onto the Loup fork among the Pawnees without losing a single one. "The Fox" admitted, however, that even in an expedition so successful as the one which he recalled there were a great many courage-testing inconveniences and annoyances. But he dwelt particularly upon the fact that the Cheyennes always kept their ponies in a corral which was in the very center of their village. The huts, habitations, tipis, and wigwams of the owners of the ponies were all constructed around their communal corral in a sort of a circle, but "The Fox" said that he nevertheless, in his individual excursion of which he proudly boasted, crawled during the middle of the night in among the ponies and was about to slip a lariat on the bell-mare without her stirring, when she gave a little jump, and the bell on her neck rang out pretty loudly. Then he laid down in the center of the herd and kept still, very still, while the horses walked over him and tramped upon him until he found it very unpleasant. But very soon he saw and heard some of the Cheyennes come out and look and walk about to see if anything was wrong. Then he said he had to stay still and silent under the horses' hoofs and make no noise, or die and surely be scalped. At last, however, the Cheyennes, one after another, all went back to their wigwams to sleep, and then he very slowly and without a sound took the bell off from the mare, put his lariat on her neck quietly, led her out and all the herd of Cheyenne ponies followed. He never stopped until he was safe up north of the Platte river and had all his equine spoils safe in the valley of the Loup fork going towards the Pawnee village where Genoa now stands.

"The Fox" declared that the number of horses he made requisition for at that time on the stables of the Cheyennes was three hundred. At this statement some incredulity was shown by Mr. Heth, myself, and some others present. Immediately "The Fox" threw back his woolen blanket which was ornamented on the inside with more than two hundred small decorative designs of horses. Among the Pawnees, and likewise, if I remember rightly, among the Otoes and Omahas, robes and blankets were thus embellished and so made to pass current as real certificates of a choice brand of character for their wearers. Each horse depicted on the robe was notice that the owner and wearer had stolen such horse. Finally, after expressions of friendship and good will, the expedition in charge of "The Fox" bade us adieu and briskly walked southward on their mission for getting horses away from their traditional enemies.

It is perhaps worth while to mention that, it being in the autumn of the year, all these Indians were carefully and deftly arrayed in autumn-colored costumes. Their blankets, head-gear and everything else were the color of dead and dried prairie grass. This disguise was for the purpose of making themselves as nearly indistinguishable as possible on the brown surface of the far-stretching plains. For then the weeds and grasses had all been bleached by the fall frosts.

In due time we reached Fort Kearny and after a pleasant and most agreeable visit with Mr. Heth and his family, Colonel Alexander and Lieutenant Bush, I pushed on alone for the Missouri river, by the North Platte route, bringing home with me two or three turkeys and a quarter of buffalo meat.

About the second evening, as I remember it, I arrived at the agency of the four bands of the Pawnee on the Loup fork of the Platte river, near where the village of Genoa in Nance county now stands. Judge Gillis of Pennsylvania was the U. S. government agent then in charge of that tribe, and Mr. Allis was his interpreter. There I experienced the satisfaction of going leisurely and observingly through the villages of the four bands of Pawnees, which there made their habitation. The names of the four confederate bands of Pawnee Indians were Grand Pawnee, Wolf Pawnee, Republican Pawnee, and Tapage Pawnee. At that time they all together numbered between four thousand and five thousand.

Distinguished among them for fearlessness and impetuous courage and constant success in war was an Indian who had been born with his left hand so shrunken and shriveled that it looked like the contracted claw of a bird. He was celebrated among all the tribes of the plains as "Crooked Hand, the Fighter." Hearing me express a wish for making the acquaintance of this famous warrior and scalp accumulator, Judge Gillis and Mr. Allis kindly volunteered to escort me to his domicile and formally introduce me. We took the trail which lay across Beaver creek up into the village. This village was composed of very large, earthen, mound-like wigwams. From a distance they looked like a number of great kettles turned wrong side up on the prairie. Finally we came to the entrance of the abode of Crooked Hand. He was at home. I was presented to him by the interpreter, Mr. Allis. Through him, addressing the tawny hero who stood before me, I said:

"It has come to my ears that you are and always have been a very brave man in battle. I have made a long journey to see you and to shake the hand of a great warrior."

This seemed to suit his bellicose eminence and to appeal to his barbaric vanity. Consequently I continued, saying: "I hear that you have skillfully killed a great many Sioux and that you have kept the scalp of each warrior slain by you. If this be true, I wish you would show me these trophies of your courage and victories?"

Immediately Crooked Hand reached under a sort of rude settee and pulled out a very cheap traveling trunk, which was locked. Then taking a string from around his neck he found the key thereunto attached, inserted it in the lock, turned it, and with gloating satisfaction threw back the lid of the trunk. It is fair to state that, notwithstanding Mr. Crooked Hand's personal adornments in the way of paint, earrings, and battle mementoes, he was evidently not a man of much personal property, for the trunk contained not one other portable thing except a string of thirteen scalps. This he lifted out with his right hand and held up before me as a connoisseur would exhibit a beautiful cameo—with intense satisfaction and self-praise expressed in his features.

The scalps were not large, averaging not much more in circumference than a silver dollar (before the crime of 1873). Each scalp was big enough to firmly and gracefully retain the scalplock which its original possessor had nourished. Each scalp was neatly lined with flaming red flannel and encircled by and stitched to a willow twig just as boys so stretch and preserve squirrel skins. Then there was a strong twine which ran through the center of each of the thirteen scalps leaving a space of something like three or four inches between each two.

After looking at these ghastly certificates of prowess in Indian warfare I said to the possessor: "Do you still like to go into fights with the Sioux?" He replied hesitatingly:

"Yes, I go into the fights with the Sioux but I stay only until I can kill one man, get his scalp and get out of the battle."

Then I asked: "Why do you do this way now, and so act differently from the fighting plans of your earlier years when you remained to the end of the conflict?" Instantly he replied and gave me this aboriginal explanation:

"You see, my friend, I have only one life. To me death must come only once. But I have taken thirteen lives. And now when I go into battle there are thirteen chances of my being killed to one of my coming out of the fight alive."

My last buffalo hunt was finished and its trophies and its choicest memories safely stored for exhibition or reminiscence at Arbor Lodge. More than thirty-seven years afterwards I am permitted this evening by your indulgence and consideration to attempt faintly to portray the country and its primitive condition at that time in that particular section of Nebraska which is now Franklin county. . . .

Slow Bull—
Oglala Sioux

About fifty in this photograph, Slow Bull had been a seasoned warrior from the age of fourteen when he fought against the Apsaroke in Red Cloud's party. In his lifetime he had fifty-five battles with the Apsaroke, Shoshone, Ute, Pawnee, Blackfoot and Kutenai. On one occasion when charging an enemy, his horse stepped in a hole and fell, the Apsaroke warrior leaping upon him. Slow Bull struck with his bow and sprang on another horse as a second Apsaroke attacked him. Slow Bull dispatched him with his hatchet, swung around and killed the first attacker.

Crow braves
returning with horses after raid

The Apsaroke was one of the most fearless of tribes and stories of raiding parties, large and small, are almost endless in number.

Indian travois

The Bullwhacker

"A curious character of overland life," wrote Henry T. Williams in the *Pacific Tourist* in 1879, "when the plains are covered with teams and long trains of freight wagons, is the bullwhacker. He is in size and shape usually of very large proportions; very strong, long, unkempt hair, and face covered with the stiffest of beards. Eight or ten yoke of oxen are usually attached to each wagon, and often two wagons are doubled up; i.e., the tongue of the second wagon passed under the body of the one ahead and was securely fastened. By the side of his wagon hangs his trusty axe and ready rifle, and on the tops of the wagons are spread the red blankets used for their cover at night.

"Of the bullwhacker it is said that his oath and his whip are both the longest ever known. The handle of the ordinary whip is not more than three feet in length, but the lash, which is of braided rawhide, is seldom less than twenty feet long. From the wooden handle, the lash swells gradually out for about six feet, where it is nearly ten inches in circumference (the point called the 'belly'); from here it tapers to within a foot of the end, which terminates in the form a ribbon-shaped thong. This is called by some facetiously a 'persuader,' and under its influence it will make the ox team progress at the magic rate of twenty miles per day. The effect on a refractory ox is quite forcible. The lazy one occasionally receives a reminder in the shape of a whack in the flank that causes him to double up as if seared with a red-hot iron.

"The bullwhacker is astonishingly accurate in throwing his lash. One of his favorite pastimes is to cut a coin from the top of a stick stuck loosely in the earth. If the coin is knocked off without disturbing the stake, it is his; if the stake is disturbed, the lash thrower loses the value of the coin. A curious incident is told of a bullwhacker noted for his accuracy. He bet a comrade a pint of whisky that he could cut the cloth on the back of his pantaloons without touching the skin beneath. The bet was accepted. The individual put himself in position, stooping over to give fair chance. The blow was delivered carefully but in earnest, and theron ensued the tallest jump on record. The owner being minus a portion of his skin, as well as a large portion of his breeches, heard the bullwhacker's sorrowful cry: 'Hell, I've lost my whisky!'"

Sun Dance Ceremony

Red Hand—Sioux

Chapter Seventeen

SLAUGHTER of the PAWNEES

O<small>N</small> A<small>PRIL</small> 5, 1873, I arrived at Plum Creek, now Lexington, with what was called the second colony from Philadelphia, Pennsylvania. Capt. F. J. Pearson, who was in charge, later became editor of the *Pioneer*. Judge Robert B. Pierce and the Tucker family were also with this colony. On our arrival the only town we found was a mile east of the present site of Lexington. It consisted of a section house, a small shanty called the Johnson restaurant, one story and a half log house run by Daniel Freeman as a general store, and a stockade built of ties used as a place of safety for the horses and cows. The upper story of the Freeman building was occupied by the Johnson family who partitioned it off with blankets to accommodate the immigrants, and the only lights we could depend upon were candle dips from the Freeman store at twenty-five cents each. At this time bread was sold at twenty-five cents per loaf.

There was also an immigrant house 20 x 40 feet located on the north side of the railroad nearly opposite the other buildings referred to. This house was divided into rooms 6 x 8 feet square with a hall between. The front room was used as Dawson County's first office by John H. MacColl, then county clerk. There was also a cow shed and water tank on the south side of the track. The depot was a mile west on a railroad section where the town was finally built.

The reason for the change of townsite was a fight between Freeman against the Union Pacific company. Freeman owned the quarter section of government land on which the buildings referred to were located.

The first house in Plum Creek was built by Robert Pierce whose famliy got permission to live in a freight car while the house was being built. While in the freight car the family was attacked by measles. In order to gain entrance to this temporary residence, a step-ladder had to be used and in visiting the family while in the car, I would find them first at one end of the switch and next at the other, and would have to transfer the ladder each time. Later on Robert Pierce was elected probate judge and served until by reason of his age he retired.

Tudor Tucker built the first frame house on Buffalo creek five mlies northeast of town. The first store building in Plum Creek was built by Mr. Betz. The first hotel was built by E. D. Johnson, who deserves much credit for his work in building up Dawson

This personal recollection of Wm. H. Brancroft, M.D., appeared under the title "Plum Creek (Lexington) Nebraska" in N<small>EBRASKA</small> P<small>IONEER</small> R<small>EMINIS-</small> <small>CENCES</small>, *Nebraska Society of Daughters of the American Revolution.*

Ready for a winter battle—Crow

This photograph was made in a narrow valley of the Pryor Mountains in Montana. It was not uncommon for the Crows to move against an enemy in the dead of winter. Brave on the left wears a hooded overcoat of blanket material adopted after the arrival of traders.

county. In 1873 the population numbered about 175. The old townsite was soon abandoned and the town of Plum Creek on its present site became a reality.

The completion of the Platte river bridge was celebrated July 4, 1873, by a big demonstration. It then became necessary to get the trade from the Republican Valley, Plum Creek being the nearest trading point for that locality. Since there were no roads from the south, a route had to be laid out. With this object in view, Judge Pierce, E. D. Johnson, Elleck Johnson, and I constituted ourselves a committee to do the work. We started across the country and laid up sod piles every mile until we reached the Arapahoe, 18 miles southwest. Coming back we shortened up the curves. This was the first road from the south into Plum Creek, and we derived a great amount of trade from this territory. It was no uncommon thing for the Erwin & Powers Company, conducting a general store at this time, to take in from one thousand to twelve hundred dollars on Saturdays. . . .

On this Sunday afternoon about five o'clock the great April storm started with blizzard from the northwest. It was impossible for any of us to get away until Tuesday afternoon. On Monday night Captain Stuckey, Doc Mellenger, and I had to take the one bed. During the night the bed broke down and we lay until morning huddled together to keep from freezing. Mellenger and I left Tuesday afternoon, when the storm abated, and started back toward the old town. The storm again caught us and drifted us to Doc's old doby two and one-half miles north of the townsite. By this time the snow had drifted from four to five feet in depth. The horses took us to the dugout stable in which we put them. Then we had to dig our way to the doby where we remained from Tuesday evening until Thursday morning. We had nothing to eat during that time but a few hard biscuits, a little bacon, and three frozen chickens, and nothing but melted snow to drink. The bedstead was a home-made affair built of pine boards. This we cut up and used for fuel and slept on the dirt floor. The storm was so terrific that it was impossible to get to the well, fifteen feet from the doby. We became so thirsty from the snow water that Doc thought he would try to get to the well. He took a rope and pistol, tied the rope around his waist and started for the well. His instructions were that if I heard the pistol I was to pull him in. After a very short time the pistol report came and I pulled and pulled and Doc came tumbling in without pistol or bucket. It was so cold he had nearly frozen his hands. Thursday was clear and beautiful. One of the persons from Mullen's, having gone to town, reported that we had left there Tuesday afternoon. On account of this report a searching party was sent out to look for us.

Another item of interest was the Pawnee and Sioux massacre on August 5, 1873. It was the custom of the Pawnees, who were friendly and were located on a reservation near Columbus, Nebraska, to go on a fall hunt for buffalo meat for their winter use. The Sioux, who were on the Pine Bluff reservation, had an old grudge against the Pawnees and knew when this hunt took place. The Pawnees made Plum Creek their starting point across the country northwest of the head of the Frenchman river. They camped about ten miles northwest of Culbertson, a town on the B. & M. railroad. The camp was in the head of a pocket which led from a tableland to the Republican river. The Sioux drove a herd of buffalo on the Pawnees while the latter were in camp. Not suspecting danger the Pawnees began to kill the buffalo, when the Sioux came up, taking them by surprise. The Pawnees, being outnumbered, fled down the canyon. The Sioux followed on either bank and cross-fired them, killing and wounding about a hundred. I was sent by the government with Mr. Longshore, the Indian agent of Columbus, and two guides to the scene of the massacre, which was about one hundred and forty miles southwest of Plum Creek, for the purpose of looking after the wounded who might have been left behind. We made this trip on horseback. The agent had the dead buried and we followed up the wounded. We found twenty-two at Arapahoe and ten or fifteen had left and started on the old Fort Kearny trail. We brought the twenty-two wounded to Plum Creek, attended to their wounds and then shipped them in a box car to the reservation at Columbus.

My first trip to Wood river valley twenty miles north, was to attend James B. Mallott, one of the first settlers. They were afraid to let me go without a guard but I had no fear of the Indians, so they gave me a belt of cartridges and a Colt's revolver. Finally MacColl, the county clerk, handed me a needle gun and commanded me to get back before dark. I started on horseback with this arsenal for Wood river and made the visit, but on my return I stopped to let the horse rest and eat bluestem. Soon the horse became frightened and began to paw and snort. On looking back toward the divide, I saw three Indians on horseback were heading my way. We were not long in getting started. I beat them by a mile to the valley, arriving safely at Tucker's farm on Buffalo creek. The Indians did not follow but rode along the foothills to the west. A party of four or five from Tucker's was not long in giving chase, but the Indians had disappeared in the hills. A little later, Anton Abel, who lived a mile north of town, came in on the run and stated that a file of eight or ten Indians, with scalp sticks waving, were headed south a half mile west of town. A number mounted their horses and gave chase to the river where the Indians crossed and were lost sight of. We never suffered much loss or injury from the Indians. Many scares were reported, but like the buffalo after 1874-75, they were a thing of the past in our country.

My practice for the first ten or twelve years among the sick and injured, covered a field almost unlimited. I was called as far north as Broken Bow in the Loup valley, fifty miles, east to Elm Creek, Buffalo county, twenty miles, west to Brady Island, Lincoln county, thirty-five miles, and south to the Republican river. Most of the time there were no roads or bridges. The valley of the Platte in Dawson county is now the garden spot of the state. As stated before the settlement of 1872 was on the extreme edge of the frontier. Now we have no frontier. It is progressive civilization from coast to coast. I have practiced my profession for over forty year continuously in this state, and am still in active practice. I have an abiding faith that I shall yet finish up with an airship in which to visit my patients.

Gwo-wot giving medicine to young brave

Photo courtesy U. of Wyoming

For Further Reading

The Fighting Cheyennes, George Bird Grinnell

The Sod House Frontier, Everett Dick

A Sioux Chronicle, George E. Hyde

My Sixty Years on the Plains, W. T. Hamilton

War Path and Bivouac, John T. Finerty

Frontier Photographer, Wesley R. Hurt and William E. Lass

South Pass 1868, James Chisholm's Journal edited by Lola M. Homsher

Early Days Among the Cheyennes, John E. Seger

Across The Wide Missouri, Bernard De Voto

The Year of Decision, Bernard De Voto

The Buffalo Hunters, Marie Sandoz

Cheyenne Autumn, Marie Sandoz

Crazy Horse, Marie Sandoz

Pawnee, Blackfoot and Cheyenne, George Bird Grinnell

Following the Indian Wars, Oliver Knight

A Tour of The Prairies, Washington Irving

These Were The Sioux, Marie Sandoz

Warpath and Cattle Trail, Herbert E. Collins

A Warrior Who Fought With Custer, Thomas B. Marquis

Recollections of the Sioux Massacre, Oscar Garrett Wall

Conquering the Mighty Sioux, William J. Bordeaux

Credits

The Sawyer Expedition from *Pioneering In The Northwest, Niobrara-Virginia City Wagon Road* by Albert M. Holman. Dietch and Lamar Co., Sioux City, Iowa, 1924; Nebraska State Historical Society.

Wounded Knee by George E. Bartlett; Ricker Collection, Nebraska State Historical Society.

Sioux and Their Customs, reprinted from the Omaha *Bee;* Ricker Collection, Nebraska State Historical Society.

To Take a Scalp by Everett L. Ellis, *Annals of Wyoming,* Vol. 31, October 1959, No. 2; Wyoming State Archives and Historical Department.

Dull Knife's Cheyenne Raid of 1878 by A. N. Keith from *Nebraska History,* Vol. 7, No. 4; Nebraska State Historical Society.

Slaughter of the Pawnees by William M. Bancroft, M.D.; The Freemans and the Frontier (First Settlers of Dawson County) by Mrs. Daniel Freeman; My Last Buffalo Hunt by J. Sterling Morton — all from *Nebraska Reminiscences,* Nebraska Society of the Daughters of the American Revolution, Nebraska State Historical Society.

Ab-Sa-Ra-Ka from *Ab-Sa-Ra-Ka* by Mrs. Margaret Irvin (Sullivant) Carrington, Lippincott's, 1868. Council Bluffs Public Library.

Indian Notes on the Custer Battle from *Indian Notes on the Custer Battle* by David F. Barry, edited by Usher L. Burdick; The Proof Press, Baltimore, 1937. Nebraska State Historical Society.

Grim Days With the Indians, A Ride for Liniment and Life and Indian Retribution, from "Incidents in the Life of Norris Griggs" by Mrs. Helen Sargent in *Annals of Wyoming,* Vol. 25, January 1953, No. 1. Wyoming State Archives and Historical Department.

Attack on Fort Laramie, Battle With the Indians at Plum Creek and Battle of Summit Springs, all from *Pacific Tourist* by Henry T. Williams, 1879.

INDEX